MW01502936

FRAGMENTS

OF THIS ABSORBING WORLD

C. A. Wynem

WITH WOOD ENGRAVINGS BY
HERBERT WATERS

STEPHEN DAYE PRESS : BRATTLEBORO, VT.

COPYRIGHT, 1941, BY STEPHEN DAYE PRESS, INC.

PRINTED IN THE UNITED STATES OF AMERICA

A VALIANT ADVENTURING SPIRIT

Is there anything that means so much in human existence as eager participation in the myriad-sided world around us? Is there anything that we so often forget in the crowding pressure of making a living, anything that we may more wisely seek?

To adventure, to see and hear and feel with the senses of the body, to comprehend with those of the mind, to thrill with those of the spirit—this is the birthright of a human being.

The perfection of a raindrop, the infinity of the stars, the tender mystery of an unfolding flower, the surge of storms in space, the age-long growth of a mountain, the rhythm of electrons in an atom, the measured march of the tides—all these and a thousand more crowd about us. To seek them, to discover their beauty of form and movement, to look deeply into their mystery, is to enter a boundless kingdom. To forget them is to exchange the richness of a full and matchless life for the poverty of a meagre existence.

CRUCIBLES

Where the laggard waters of the fleeing tide
Linger by the bleak seaside
When the night is o'er,
Resting on the sloping shore,
Leaving in the soft, black ooze
Pools that timid shellfish choose,
Pools that stranded seaforms share,
Waiting for the tide, and where
Shadows of an early wing
Pass like some faint, ghostly thing,
There at dawn the amber ray,
First to whisper "Day!",
Seeking cupels for its grace,
Falls and turns to gold in each, still, shallow place.

RUNAWAY

My train has just passed a stream that is out of its banks. A stream shows a wholly new mood when it does that, I think. It's a runaway. Its usual inhibitions are temporarily submerged and it wilfully and freely does what it secretly desires to do all the rest of its days but never quite succeeds in doing. It reveals its hidden aspirations. No wonder it is interesting! Perhaps if it could not do that once in a while in its lifetime it would get so deep down within its usual banks that it could never venture—never discover new ways to new places.

POLAND

I went to see about andirons. The man who makes them (he makes gates and finer things for more important people) is a Pole. He is a splendid craftsman. You would glory in his personal pride in his own fingers' work. He is native to Poland, native to its soil. Behind his shop he has an assortment of affairs that delighted me—a dove-cote, a hen-yard, a duck pool, a rabbitry, a goldfish pond, a dog house, some guinea pigs, and a flower garden. He took me "through" them all. Round about there were factories and unsightly dumps, but behind his workshop was his bit of soil, a bit of Poland. You would enjoy the man.

He uses quaint, homeland expressions. "Grandfather orders, grandson gets" was his phrase to show the slowness of hand-work, with which the Americans have no patience.

I spent an hour and a half with him, and left there with a conflicting bunch of zinnias.

A nice spot in the day.

SHADOWS

A day of rare shadows—

The shadows of little wings as the owners flew across the road; shadows of clouds from a sky that was truly the abode of some giant who governs those glorious grey and white bits of wonder; shadows under stream banks. Trees pictured in lakes. And those soul-delighting shadows that drift with sunlight through the woods, across tree trunks and branches.

A wonderfully rare day.

BY HAND

I do not know how much there is of spiritual imagination and of intangible appreciations in the usual pioneer. Often, I suspect, those inner senses are not especially developed—and often necessarily they are buried or crushed under the weight of bodily necessities.

Sometimes those whom one talks with in the remoter places seem to look about with eyes that see the invisible,—and sometimes they seem to be aware only of that which is concrete and "practical."

But if those who hew out their homes in such places could be free enough of dire necessity, both inwardly and outwardly, I should think that one of the rarest experiences of a whole life-time would be to create an abiding place literally with one's own hands, from the ground up—the logs from the trees, the fireplace and chimney from rocks, the chairs, table—all, piece by piece, a little at a time, each separate article representing when finished a careful, absorbing selection and fashioning, each as individual and as full of personality as if it were a living creature. What extraordinary associations there would be in all of the details of such a place.

Something like that is surely behind the joy that one finds in possessing or even in looking at the things that have come down to us from earlier ages and those that are fashioned by unmechanized people today.

When a simple people become infected with the ways and products of "civilization"—when they buy ready-made what they used to make themselves—*what a loss to the world* it is!

BEYOND

Untamed wood road, I'll never know
What lies ahead, around your bend.
I'll never see the dim spot where you end.
My eager steps trod just a little way
And then I heard the call to come away.
Your snaring raspberry vines,
Your dwarfed, misshapen, windworn pines,
The drooping, frosted goldenrod,
That one white ripening milkweed pod,
The lichened green-rock wall,
I saw them all!
But just beyond, I know,
Had swift time let me go,
I should have found, around that bend
And at your far-off, far-off end,
A magic, lyric waterfall,
Some wild bird's questioning call,
A glint of captured gold,
In Cambrian rock so old, so old.
I should have felt the lure divine
Of Northland bush, and heard the whine
Of winds through pointed fir.
Perhaps I should have heard the whirr
Of patridge wings in fearless flight,
And caught rare broken rays of woodland light
If I had gone beyond, around the bend,
And on, and on, to your dim fading end.

COSMIC LIGHT

Do you know that when there is no moon the dim light at night is only partly from the stars? Only about a fourth of it. More than half is from cosmic rays—think of that! About fifteen percent is glow from faroff, hidden aurora. Isn't that wonderful?

Maybe the woods animals that can move about so securely in the dark have eyes that are especially sensitive to cosmic rays. Maybe many insects are similarly equipped.

CAMP-FIRE

To me there is something very personal about a camp-fire, large or small. To build it is like creating life and to tend it is like nuturing life. I feel like giving to it the best that I know how, and in return I expect of it to be all that it can be. To bring it into being carelessly is somehow, to me, to do an unworthy thing. In some very definite way it hurts. I like a fire to be prepared far in advance, its place in the world thoughtfully chosen, its fibre and substance planned, its making alight almost a rite, because for a time it is going to be the center of a new world.

All through its life it *is* a center. As far as its light and warmth extend it creates its own universe. Beyond its living circle the rest of the world grows dim and unimportant, as the rest of the world should.

If it were a fire on a hearth I should almost wish to retain some glowing coal alive through all time—to cover a big ember with beautiful grey ashes and thus hold to the life of it through any period when it must be left alone for a while.

Always I have wished not to quench a fire that I have built. To cause the fire to cease to exist seems always like bringing a good and useful life to an end.

A NEW WORLD

Some time I want to watch little plants and birds and all the things and creatures of some spot from a point close to *the ground*—with eyes down in the midst of grass blades and weed-stems. I want to see that world in that way.

EARLY HOURS

I can never agree with all the great multitude who look upon early morning hours as in themselves something to be avoided and slept through and complained about if tasted. I have never in my life felt anything other than a great welcome for sunrise and the coming of day—a sense of adventure in being about in the first hours of dawn and growing light and activity.

This seems to be a prime time of year for birds that hunt their food on tree trunks and limbs. A black and white creeper has been investigating my trees along with the woodpeckers. He goes in a straighter course up the trunk, in little even jerks or jumps, and doesn't dodge around so much.

Don't you suppose that now is the time when a trunk or limb is especially well stocked with bugs? I think so. They have been hiding in crevices for several weeks now, ready for their long Winter sleep. There must be a lot of them, all told. To a creeper or a woodpecker the Fall must be a season when the dinner table is nicely fat and when a meal can be achieved in pleasantly short order. Think what fun it must be to explore a big tree-trunk and continually to find excellent little grubs of all sorts of nice flavor! There must be a series of delectable finds every hour, each one a surprise in its way.

Later, I suppose, when Winter is well along and the territory has been searched repeatedly and no new grubs are being produced to fill the gaps, the picking must grow scanty—like reaching into a bag in which there has been a large bunch of grapes and finding only bare stems and a few inferior little fruits down in the bottom in the midst of the debris.

COMMUNION

In the tabernacle of a lonely bay
I found, enshrined 'mid green pine trees,
A mountain ash in fruit that in its way
Became a chalice, proffering its cup
Of scarlet beauty to the eye
For rare communion with the All of All.
And I, a pilgrim passing by,
Partook, within the cloister of that bay,
Of all the tree held forth to me.
I drank the sacred wine and went away.

THE TIGHTENING CIRCLE

Even here in New York today the air is splendidly clear and fresh. I think that winds must have dipped to the surface of the ocean many miles off shore and then risen high and remained aloft until some descending current carried them into the city streets. They have a quality that is not of stone and bricks and crowding humanity but of wide spaces and of clean and cold water.

What a strange circle human beings have got themselves into— an always widening and yet always tightening circle! In front of a window a little while ago I saw a silent crowd watching a girl feed

spinach leaves into a machine. A motor within it turned some concealed mechanism and out from the machine came a green juice that flowed into a glass jug labelled "Juice-o-veg. Spinach," while out from another orifice came twisting green dry shreds. Drink the juice and you got the equivalent of spinach, they said. From other jugs you could imbibe carrots or peas or whatnot.

So here, in these few square miles, four or five million persons, living in their Park Avenue apartments or in their East Side warrens, tearing through the streets in their taxicabs or crowding into their hot roaring subway cars, defeating every normal manner of life and substituting an always widening and tightening circle of abnormal living, could now go to the corner store and buy pseudo-normality in a glass jug. More crowding, more speed, more noise—and constantly more and more effort to counteract the consequences.

I don't know whether the spinach juice represented technically and biologically the essential spinach content, but I think that buying a glass jug and drinking the juice is a long way from roaming the woods and plains, finding the wild plants that grow there and eating the leaves or gnawing the root. I think that some living vital quality of the freshly gathered plant can never be squeezed out alive by a machine and bottled in a jug. Perhaps the carbohydrates are there and the vitamins and the minerals, but not the beating heart of the plant nor the rippling muscles and tanned skin of the human being who searches for it, nor the quick eye and the alert mind that goes to find it and makes good in the quest.

PRODIGALITY

How prodigal a plant is with its individual blossoms! I brought back with me a single spray of golden rod, one of meadowsweet, and one of Queen Anne's lace. Each one I selected as representing ordinary size. Then I counted the tiny blossoms on a single branchlet of each and from that estimated the rest.

The Queen Anne's lace had about twenty-five little blossoms on each segment and there were twenty-five segments. Think of it— six hundred and twenty-five perfect little blossoms! Besides these there were nine or ten segments at the center that were smaller. Say seven hundred all told. And this was only one blossom-cluster. There were others on the same plant.

The golden rod had ninety-four individual yellow blossoms on one segment of its graceful bloom, and there were fifteen segments. More than fourteen hundred for this one "bloom."

The tiny blossoms that make up the meadowsweet's cluster are exquisite. Crinkly petals of a delicate pink shade and fantastic, curved stamens. There were about twenty of these to a little sub-cluster, ten of those to a segment, and ten segments to the whole "flower."

CENTURIES PAST

Centuries past on a mist-swept isle,
Stretched prone 'neath the pall of the sky,
A lonely and wind-whipped figure stood,
A soul—called "I."

Salty tears from the surf off shore
Were blown to her loosened hair
And mingled with moisture on her lips
While she—stood there.

Gannets, gulls, with their wings of steel
Cast shadows of flight on the hill.
They lingered a while and then sped on
While she—stood still.

Dusk—and at last came the island night,
All dark where the sea grass grew.
The wings and the waves were stilled in sleep
And she—slept too.

OCTOBER

These October days, are they not beautiful! The ripe rich quality of the air, the warm glow of the colors, the tang of the odors, the competent self-reliant approach of all living things toward the coming winter that seems to me to say "See!—My house is snug and tight, my stores to carry me through snow and cold are complete and in order."

All of it appeals to something deep within me. I like it, like to walk on and on in the midst of it, like to think of the sparkle of the stars and of dry wood under cover and of the warmth and light of a wood fire sending up its flames and sparks and smoke and settling down to glowing luminous coals that grow only the more beautiful as the hours slip by.

There is so much of loveliness and beauty in this world of ours, so much to see and hear and smell and touch—all of it always new, always more and more delightful as understanding grows.

JUNK

On my way to town this morning I went through a street devoted solely to junk. I was interested in the business signs appearing there.

There was "The . . . . Salvage Co.", "The . . . . Rebuilt Co.", "The . . . . Reclaiming Co.". I find that old rags on this street become among other things "wiper cloths." Once in a long distance a sign "The . . . . Junk Co." appeared, but not often. The word "junk" is avoided. It apparently offends the ears and eyes of the aesthetic dealers in discarded commodities. Undoubtedly it is only the simple soul or the dealer whose wife and children have few social ambitions who dares to call his business one of junk.

I am fascinated with that street. It is crowded with small offices and large yards. The yards are filled with discarded automobiles, motors, engines, and anything and everything of metal value. There, under scant shelters, are bales upon bales of bundled rags, all sorted by kind and color. A bad ending, isn't it, for a proud motor car or a particularly alluring negligee!

RAIN

This morning just after I had stepped out of bed I heard rain pattering on the broad green burdock leaves beneath my window. I liked it. I always do. I like to hear it, enjoy the feel of it, enjoy the quality of the air when rain comes, its freshness and its moist cleanness. And I think that there is something else in it that gives pleasure, some sense of refreshment, some intangible feeling of joy in meeting weather on its own terms and finding it good.

WITHDRAWAL

I have just been out to walk down the driveway and feel the cool air and look up at the countless stars. Very bright and beautiful they are tonight.

It would be a rare and wonderful privilege to be on some mountain top where no other light than that of the sky could be discerned, where no sound came except the murmur of little woods creatures or of birds stirring in their sleep, where the air was as clean as the sky itself. I think that it would be possible there to withdraw in thought and spirit into the depths of the universe—to touch and feel and to understand a little the inner being of life, to gain perspective on years and centuries.

Withdrawal—removal from confusion and stress and conflict— this is the cry of so many folk these days. The times seem to emphasize it more than ever before in my memory—or at least I hear the cry more insistently. Surely it discloses a need. But I think too that it points to a resource.

PLANET

Again, that blazing, magnificent, personal morning star!

It was just before dawn when I looked out and up to see it. Vast misty greyness over the breadth of the field, the tracery of leafless bushes near by (the dark columns of tree trunks giving them background), the grey misty distance merging into a deep band of darker grey cloud, very far off, and that in turn giving way imperceptibly to a brighter band—and over that the glorious star, its fires well tended and burning with a living flame!

I saw the first rose tints come up above the horizon.

Later, as the light in the East grew, the star did what it always does—slowly took on its changed, temporarily changed, tone and degree of illumination in preparation for the day of the sun's dominance and of human mundane activity.

It seems to me that as the light grows this star becomes aloof from the rest of the world, imperial, secluded. It does not fade. Its light grows whiter, less warm, more remote, impersonal in relation to the ordinary comings and goings of men. It retires into some high domain in the heavens to wait there, regal, intense, until the vast movement of the earth will again dim the skies, send men to sleep, and thus prepare a place where a being of such glory may fittingly return to those who know it and understand.

SALLY'S PRAYER

Dear Lord of all the World,
Please let it be
That I—a little girl—
Shall ever see
The soft, green leaves upon each tree
And always hear
When small birds sing quite near.
Please let me love
The moon and stars that glow above
And let me feel
That all the shining sea
Is made, dear Lord, by thee for me!

INDIAN CHILDREN

We stopped at a port where there is an Indian village. Very small Indian children were playing in the midst of driftwood on the beach. The boys were self-possessed, as if they were old Indians who had dropped all their years except five or six, but still retained some of the experience and poise of age,—poise combined with the energy and playfulness of youth. There was a certain harmless toughness about them that was both of age and of youth, principally evidenced by an expert spitting. Two little girls were imperturbable. One of them remained serenely unresponsive to anything I might say or do. The other was cast in the same mold but with a chink in her armor. Twice she suddenly burst into wiggling smiles.

All of them were quite free from self-assertion or noisy ways. I suppose that they are a trial to their parents at times. But they were no nuisance to strangers.

CROW

How sophisticated, crafty-minded, worldly-wise is the crow, as compared with many other birds! His instincts and habits seem to have in them no touch whatever of imagination, of simple spontaneity.

Every morning and from time to time through the day crows are here and there in the region around my cabin. Sometimes they are quite silent, but if you see them and observe them closely you will find that there is deliberate design in their silence—it is never the quiet of repose or contemplation. Often they are engaged in noisy uproar, yelling from one treetop to another, swearing at the top of their lungs at the gray squirrels, or seemingly making a loud noise for the sake of making it, like hoodlums in a vacant city lot.

Robins spend hours singing their song from some elevated branch where they can face the dawn or the setting sun or just the world in general. At such times they seem to be entirely filled with the spirit of song, with an overflowing joy in being alive. They seem unaware of the ordinary business of life, untouched by the prosy needs for food and the other necessities of permanent robin existence. They are suffused with a glow of enthusiasm.

But I can not imagine a crow's ever sharing such a feeling. He seems forever at war with the universe.

Robins thrive in spite of their unworldliness. They build their nests in absurdly exposed and vulnerable situations. They walk about without fear in search of food. They stand upon a roof-top and sing for a solid half-hour with never a care, apparently, as to any enemy.

A crow places its nest in so inaccessible, so hidden, a situation that few persons ever see its crude mass. It hunts food with eyes so warily alert that nothing can move within a quarter of a mile without being noted. It arouses enmities in every quarter by a perpetual fighting attitude. It has grown so much in the habit of using its voice in hooting and jeering and yelling "Police!" that there is nothing of song left in its vocal cords.

In the bird world the crow seems to me to represent the impressive example of the logical outcome of certain human proverbs and admonishings, often quoted and urged—

"Keep an eye on the main chance."
"The Lord helps those who help themselves."
"Do others or they will do you."
"The dollar talks."
and all the rest of similar philosophy.

13

AWAKENING

Let me dine from a wild grape leaf,
Let my wine be the evening's dew,
Let me lie on a sweet grass couch,
Let the sky spread its robe of blue.

Let soft mist cool my upturned face,
Let eyes kissed by the clouds soon close,
Let pale light from the stars grow faint,
Let deep night bring me rare repose.

Let the moon weave me dreams of bliss,
Let the rune of wide space renew
All the throb of our love. And this—
Let me open my eyes to you!

APPRECIATION

Always I have liked to go early to concerts. Always I have
wished to do that. There is a certain feeling of preparedness about
it. The entry of the orchestra means anticipation and almost participation. Their tuning up is interesting—like varied birds in
woods trying out their songs. I have never liked to go late—nor
just in time. If the house was nearly empty when I arrived the
feeling of pleasure and a sort of inside participation was heightened.
Folk who came late seemed to me strangely defective and gave
me the feeling that they were defrauding themselves through some
curious lack of appreciation.

Those who prepared to leave while the closing minutes were in
progress were still worse. They had been listening to it all and for
some unaccountable reason they were willing to break in upon a
right enjoyment of the very climax. It was as if, being in possession
of a book and having read all but the last few paragraphs, they
had no more understanding than to tear out the final pages and
throw them away.

SNEEZE

This morning while my car was in traffic and waiting for the
signal to move I noticed a junk wagon with its shabby Semitic
owner on the seat and a decidedly plush horse in the traces. All
this was to my left and forward. While I was deciding that I had
not many times seen such an uneven back, such a weather-beaten
tail, and such plumed hocks on any equine, and just as I was deciding that the *complicatus* tooth was not old but was his, he
sneezed!

It was the wettest, most profound, most far-reaching sneeze I have ever witnessed (the sunshine in the air told me that). The driver in front got it all, through his open window, for the horse had turned his head to the right. Then there was another sneeze—and then one more.

All this was followed by the most lovable, most friendly, most winning of horse smiles. Even the unfortunate man before me responded. As for me I forgot where I was and laughed aloud.

Just then traffic moved. If it had not I should have become friends with that charming horse whose mother forgot to tell him to "cover" his sneezes.

WORK

I have been variously employed today—exceedingly variously. I have just finished dictating a report—a task that has its elements of interest but also is somewhat like enumerating the potatoes in a bin and classifying them as to their size and shape and the number of warts on them and the state of their sprouts.

Isn't it funny how one's work is constituted! So seldom deliberately and constructively planned, and so often a sort of automatic growth, like a limb on a tree—angular—thick or thin as the case may be—scraggly—with obscuring bark—vitalized somehow inside—bearing a little fruit if it's lucky.

VISTAS

My little woods back of my cabin! I am going to wander through them and see what I can see. They have been transformed in these last few days. When I left for the West they were in full glory of rose and scarlet dress, great sweeps and folds of it flung over every branch and twig. When I got back the robes had been dropped, all except the seal brown garments of the oaks, and there in full view stood the forms of the trees themselves, all in their native naturalness and frankness of honest trunk and vigorous limb and delicate twig. Where before I could see only a few yards into the woods because the robes were flung across my view, now I can look into distances.

I do not know which is the more alluring—the richness and fullness of the Fall garments or the revealing vistas that are now opened to view.

RESTORATION

I have been asked about creative work—about writing, about its significance and mission and the end it can attain.

There are times, I think, that cry out for the novel, the play, the essay, that seizes upon human wrongs and faults and holds them up to searing light, rousing men to strike against them.

There is place for the wrath and passion that such writing may call forth, even for the destructive and consuming fires that it may set, for the marshalling of men against men, if only from such conflict shall come a new and greater human welfare and peace.

There are times when a people have grown smug in selfish contentment, when perhaps the only force that can rouse them to a better and finer life is a destructive and terrible force.

But there are times also when the illness of the human spirit is not that of too great contentment, too willing acceptance of that which is unworthy, but is an illness of the tired and despairing spirit, the spirit that has lost its hold on eternal values, that cannot look up at the sky because its eyes have been too long fixed upon the clods and stones of the earth, that cannot hear the music of the spheres because it has been listening too long to the quarreling sounds from human throats, that cannot feel the power within itself because it has forgotten that such power exists and has spent its energy in pushing here and there, blindly, in human conflict.

These years, here and now, are a period of wearing struggle, of dimmed inspiration, of forgotten values, of dulled faith. They are not a period of sluggish contentment. This is not a time when conflict is needed.

This is a time when human beings need beauty, the light of a clear inner spark that can illuminate their own souls, the steady glow of that which will restore and set aright, the beacon to the wonders of a truly wonderful world.

This wonderful world!—That is the essence of the great need, that is the greatest of all aims now for those who have the vision for creative work.—Mystery—beauty—understanding!

ON A MOUNTAIN TRAIL

Long ago on a mountain trail
I glimpsed a fleeting coyote tail,
And knelt to see the water seep
From bear tracks freshly made and deep.
I watched an elk with frenzied push
Sweep stately horns through tangled bush.
And when the trail led over rock
Where whistling marmots came to mock,
I stood upon a summit shelf
And found a gift from Life itself.
For here, above the timber line,
The Earth below was wholly mine.

THE ONCOMING

I should like to ride on the very front of a train as it makes its way out of a network of paths of steel, such as that of the South Station. I'd like to do it at night, when hundreds of red and of violet signal lights crowd the space in front of the advancing engine. I'd like to see the ribbons of shining steel ahead, dividing and uniting, curving to right and left, and to feel the great beast with its big wheels and its heavy throb threading its purposeful way through the maze, dragging after it the string of lighted coaches. I'd like to feel the beast press forward and lunge on into space, as the engineer opened the throttle wider, and to see the lights of buildings and streets give way to open country, to trees and fields sweeping by in the dark. I think it would be an enriching experience to sense thus the might of a locomotive, to share its tearing rush through the spaces of the night.

All our lives we ride in trains and learn only what it means to be pulled along, to look out and back but never ahead, to be part of the tail and not part of the throbbing source of power that drags the tail behind it. The country that we see through windows is already vanishing when we catch sight of it. We can never anticipate and watch the oncoming. We see no forest or river or mountain until it is about to leave us.

I'd like to be able to catch first glimpses of the horizon ahead, to watch the forest and the mountain grow to full extent and stature, to advance upon them, swiftly, inexorably.

ISLANDS

I have been awake since very early indeed—up before any least daylight, unless the soft white glow in the mist was the coming of a new dawn. A morning in which treetops are all little islands rising out of a great white ocean.

CORRELATION

I like to see the finished, adroit use of the human body, the delicate correlation of muscles, the ripple of flowing strength, the smooth and perfectly timed rebound of muscular impact, the daring that has become confident assurance and certainty, the ultimate in quickness of eye and precise response of muscle.

I think that I derive almost as much pleasure from all this, when I see it in the perfection of an acrobat's skill—a tumbler, a juggler— or that of an expert marksman or a great rider—as when I am enjoying the performance of a pianist or violinist. Not quite the same of course, but certainly a definite pleasure in its way.

THE RUINS OF MUCKROSS ABBEY

My thanks to thee,
Franciscan brethren who lie dead,
That I may mediate an hour
And bow my head
Within the shadows of the abbey walls
That harboured thee—
That I may pace thy moss-grown halls!

Thy gift to me
Lies not in lichened masonry,
With all its roofless emptiness,
But in the sea
Of misty vows that surges on the strand
Of all my soul,
And bathes it with a spirit hand.

ATTAINMENT

A grey squirrel can leap an astonishing distance. I am still en-
deavoring to keep these interesting but too industrious neighbors
from getting all of the seeds intended for the birds. The covered
feeding tray, suspended from a wire between two trees in front of
my steps, had a board at one end on which seeds were placed to
let the birds know where to look. That part worked all right. But
the squirrels managed to reach the tray, even in its inaccessible
position. I saw one on it—then saw him go out on the board and
leap from its end straight across to an apple tree. Six feet in the
clear! A dozen times the length of the squirrel's body! As if a man
after taking a step or two should jump seventy feet!

I've now shortened the board two feet. I think that they can't
make it with this new handicap.

There is a new and very large squirrel nest high up in a tree a
few yards from the cabin. That makes two such nests close by.

THE CASCADES

The Cascade mountains delighted me. My train climbed into
their midst some time in the night, and I suppose had crossed their
best part, but when I looked out after daylight we were still winding about in their deeply forested slopes—and they were splendid.

They are shaggy mountains, and not to be walked up and down
in any place one might choose. The angles are too steep and the
woods are too luxuriant. The early morning clouds were shaggy
too. All of it—forests—mountains—clouds—was completely different from the Rockies. They seemed to offer remoteness, even
near the railroad. They would be good mountains to visit.

MAYANS

I have a new book on Mayan civilization. Do you know, the Aztecs and Mayans for some reason have always seemed a bit dull to me. I wonder why, for they have done things and done them well. I never think of a single light-hearted creature's ever having lived among them—which of course is wrong. I have worked out their wonderful calendar, have shuddered at their stern decorations, but I do not enjoy them. Perhaps this book will give me a new outlook.

MALEVOLENCE

I want to take a cat apart! I want to take it apart and learn what divine contrivance is responsible for those ghoulish, murderous, eerie noises and calls that issue from the innards of a cat.

Unobserved I observed at near distance two cats, nose to nose, jowls dripping, tongues every now and then palpitating—and at motionless moments those tremendous, breath-taking, hair-raising yowls! I want to know.

Think of the concentrated and unmixed malevolence that is so neatly and so charmingly expressed in that eye-to-eye glittering pose and that wonderful yowl that is emitted without one atom of apparent change or relief in the emittor! Think of the beautiful outpouring of glands that must take place to give rise to and to sustain those long minutes of pure hate! I don't care a hurrah about a cat as to its attachments of muscles, its arterial system, and all the rest that no doubt is entrancing to the laboratory enthusiast. But I am with you in wanting to know how it works inside in these absorbing exhibitions.

Tonight another sunset of gold—of coppery gold this time—a great bed of it in slanting, rippling bars, like a vast sloping beach of gold-and-copper sand, all wave-marked in endless parallel lines.

There is something about the glory of a sunset that carries me far off into a distant country, into the mountains and plateaus and mysteries of a land that is in no one tangible place but is a part of all, something that leads me to share in the spirit of a great and deep romance of earth and air and sky. I like to let my thoughts and spirit wing on and on, and I seem to find in the flight a wistful freedom, a quest and a realization, a yearning and a fulfillment. Remote countries come suddenly into sight and being. Adventure becomes actuality. The regions that I see are all new and yet half familiar. They beckon, and for the moment I can set foot on them. They are not commonplace, not worlds of routine, not dull or sordid or tinged with workaday worry, but sheer romance—romance.

A sunrise, best a winter sunrise, carries with it something of the same spirit. Away off, miles and leagues away, drama is unfolding. The sun is again coming to visit that part of the earth where I live. It is sending ahead of it glowing heralds of light, illuminating the heavens, touching with rays of growing power the farthest horizon. Stars, bright and of infinite mystery, have awaited the dawn. From a far country, down below the rim of the world, a new day is approaching. Sunset, dawn, sky, earth—united in glowing glory! What gifts they are!

CHOPIN

Upstairs in this building of mine some one was playing a piano— a Chopin waltz—as I came into my office a moment ago.

Somehow the sound of it seemed like a bit of the outdoors, of fresh and simple and graceful things, of that which is of the spirit instead of that which is of the material world.

Once in a while I hear it thus at a noon hour, or perhaps in the late afternoon. It seems to bring to a place that is dealing with pounds and centimeters, with reagents and statistics and accounts, a welcome note that is like a song.

THE ABYSS

A word, a look, a touch—
This much,
No more,
To bring me to the shore,
That distant shore,
Of your deep, inner mind
Where I may find
Your soul.

I know that when my word
Is heard
It means
Not all that's meant. It seems,
Always it seems,
To lose its inner sense
In thickets dense
Between.

My look wings on its way
To say
"Ah, friend—",
But very near the end,
The journey's end,
It fades away and dies,
And dying tries
To win.

I touch your hand and feel
A seal,
A bond,
That reaches on beyond,
Far, far beyond,
The outer, barren land
To where you stand,
Alone.

They fail, these means of mine,
Divine
Behest
Alone might end the quest,
My fruitless quest,
By bidding you reveal,
Yourself unseal,
The shrine.

Always your secret soul,
My goal,
Like some
Opaque and precious pearl,
A hidden pearl,
Will lie concealed from me.
I'll never see
Its form.

This small rabbit who loafs around under my windows—I have a notion that I could recognize him among other rabbits. He has a certain untroubled look about his eyes, and he carries his ears at an easy slant. He moves in an unhurried way. He sits with just a suggestion of slouch, and I am positive that if he were a human being he would like to slump down in a chair and repose on the base of his spine. His fur seems to look a bit ruffled or untidy in that part of his body which lies just ahead of his stubby tail. It gives me distinctly the impression that when he gets up in the morning and washes his face and hands and prepares for daylight hours, he is careless as to those parts of his attire not easily reached.

He sits and chews for long periods. It is inconceivable that there is anything remaining in his mouth to be chewed. I think that simply he is absent-minded and easy-going, and forgets that he has swallowed whatever it was that he had found.

To my notion he is a very definite rabbit. He is young Mr. So-and-So, with a family name and a given name and probably still another representing his mother, who I am sure would disapprove his tendency toward untidiness and his evident, easy-going qualities (which no doubt he inherited from that lazy but likable father of his).

I have a feeling myself that this young blade, if he manages the energy and initiative to get himself a wife, will turn out to be only thus-and-so as a husband. I cannot imagine his serving as a model and preceptor to young progeny. He'll just sit and chew and meditate.

THE CAROLINAS

These long stretches of woods down here in the Carolinas have their interest. I find a definite pleasure in watching their steadily moving panorama. I would not choose them as the best among woodland regions. They cannot for a moment compare with the forests of mountain areas, east or west, with Oregon or Colorado or California or New England. Yet they appeal to me more than the broad cultivated spaces of the central states.

In these great woods here there must be many, many little animals—raccoons, opossums, squirrels. They have big areas all nicely to themselves. Roads are only sandy trails. A darkey once a year is perhaps the only visitor. It is all about as it was, I'd think, before Columbus arrived. A through highway that I see now near the railroad merely borders a wilderness. The roads that occasionally lead from it do not invite the tourist or the usual visitor. The big swamps, too, must mean great sanctuaries for birds and small beasts.

Through some of these forests it would be good fun to ride horseback. The trees are spaced out. One could ride almost anywhere. The sandy ground and the fallen needles of the pine trees would make a silent trail. One should come upon much that is interesting.

MY FIRST CABIN

I was very young when I made my first cabin—against the backyard fence. A remarkable creation it was!—including even a built-in seat, upholstered with an old piece of carpet padded underneath with excelsior. It had a window, a single piece of glass. I remember well the long labor of sawing the hole for it, and the precarious task of nailing the strips that held the glass in place. It had a door, a single wide board with leather hinges, and some sort of catch that fastened the thing shut. The roof was quite flat, and I remember that it leaked and that I caulked it with rags and putty.

It was romance, adventure! It was miles and miles away from all the accustomed parts of the world. When I reached the end of the back yard and opened the door I stepped into another planet. When other youngsters came—or grownups, which was very seldom—I showed them my place as if it were some dwelling in a western mountain forest or some cave in a remote valley.

You see, the thing is in my blood.

EL TULE

I have just read about El Tule, a certain cypress tree of Oaxaca, Mexico. It has a circumference of 108 feet and a height of 141 feet. It is the oldest thing on earth of its kind—3,000, 5,000, 10,000 years! They do not know the age.

How much that tree has seen!

EMBERS

Yesterday a fire in the fireplace. I stretched out and watched every moment of its happy existence. It carried me off to places where I have been, high and quiet places, and it told me about enchanting spots that I have never visited.

I made clouds and rivers and canyon walls out of the embers. I watched every spark, and pictured it as coming from a camp-fire, a true camp-fire where the odors of a mountain night and of timberline trees mingled with that of burning wood. I watched the final glow until I almost drifted off to sleep "under the stars."

Just see what one small fire can do!

SATISFACTION

I have been thinking this morning of the rightful significance of work, of the gulf (the almost measureless gulf) that separates it from the actual significance as it exists today for millions.

To me it seems that work, day by day, is meant to be the expression of an inner urge, not simply toward the provision of food and shelter but toward the satisfaction of accomplishment—real, purposeful, tangible accomplishment—toward building, making, fashioning, planning, improving, completing something that that person likes to do, has learned or is learning how to do, genuinely enjoys doing, is fitted to do, is both stimulated and satisfied in doing.

MELODY

Gray sky, gray gulls, gray sea,
Breathe in silent harmony.
Rolling wave and moving wing
Together sing
A muted song
To which soft drifting clouds belong.
And thus a drear and lonely day
Becomes a melody in gray.

WINTER AND BIRDS

Out on the east side of my cabin the snow beneath the living-room window is all packed down tonight for a space of several square yards, and I think that much of it has been done by the small feet of birds. Perhaps a rabbit helped, though I have not chanced to distinguish his tracks. I could not anyway unless it would be at the edge of the packed-down space or beyond it. Perhaps a squirrel helped. But much of it has been done by birds. It looks as if a whole army had been there, as much trampled as if large animals had milled about.

I wonder if birds are reasonably comfortable through these cold nights. Of course they are warmly feathered, and as they crouch on a twig in a sheltered place, or on the ground, each becomes a ball that is all covered with a protecting layer. But this morning I noticed that an early chickadee seemed to ruffle his feathers a bit, and I wondered.

Does the winter mean a season of hardship that simply must be endured? Do the bird songs of spring and early summer mean something more than just courtship days? Do they express also the joy of a season when days and nights are more livable in creature-comforts, when food is more abundant, when the cares that are represented by shelter and warmth are more easily met and when spirits rise accordingly?

THE LADY AND THE STARS

What do some people do with their eyes and ears and brains?

A well-dressed woman, evidently much travelled, stood talking with a man on the deck of my steamer. Both were of middle age and must have had thirty or forty years in which to see and think and learn. The woman was speaking somewhat gushingly of the stars that were beginning to appear as evening drew on.

"Isn't it wonderful to think how many there are and how they shine!" she exclaimed.

"Yes," her companion assented.

"What makes them shine?" she asked.

"It's the reflection from the sun," he explained.

The lady seemed to find this quite satisfactory.

BORDERLAND

Today has been full. A bread-and-butter day. The conference was long drawn-out.

Meanwhile today subways and their crushing crowding. Hordes ramming other hordes through the doors. A ride in an automobile back to New York late this afternoon, over the elevated highway that crosses the big Jersey marshes and dives into the Holland tunnel. Armies of trucks on that, and dodging through the midst of them a lesser army of "pleasure cars."

What a strange race of beings it is that crowds together in a city like this to such extent that it must send to mines and mills for steel and concrete with which to construct a gigantic viaduct and a deep tunnel so that the hurrying throngs can get into and out of the complicated maze in which they have involved themselves.

Down beneath the viaduct miles and miles of marshes, with water-plants and tall grasses and cat-tails! Pressing upon the border of this quiet reminder of lost years the buildings and noisy streets of a frantic city!

I suppose that there must be muskrats and mice and other little animals, many of them, in the marshes. I think that in a muskratty and micey way they must look up at the viaduct and wonder—and I hope that they retire to their burrows in wise contentment.

I repeat, I hope that the muskrats and mice retire to their burrows in well justified contentment.

PROPHECY

A touch of peace enfolds the firmly woven web,
The slim cocoon, where pupal life with quiet flow and ebb
Slumbers in enchanted sleep until a quickened start
Releases power that tears the silken web apart.

Deep peace enfolds the hollow where the fatted bear,
Curled warmly, deep within his soundless winter lair,
Waits with dimly beating heart that freeing, first Spring day
When from his den he'll go in hunger on his way.

Perhaps in quiet joy deep pools of future dreams
Lie spread throughout such sleep. Perhaps there gleams
Through all the mist of all this peace and fast repose
A forecast of a life anew—a prophecy. Who knows!

WHITE CLOAKS

The whole world about here is gloriously cloaked in whiteness.
The pines are exquisitely lovely. The birds have been a little subdued today as if overwhelmed by so much falling snow.

I wonder if trees are not secretly glad to have the snow fall upon
them. There must be some trees, more vain than others, that
realize that so clad they are at the height of their beauty. There
are a few here today that seem to be preening themselves, adjust-
ing this branch and that, shedding a bit of snow now and then,
evidencing by these and by other quivers of delight that they are
glad to be part of the winter landscape.

FRIENDLY DOGS

I have been enjoying friendly dogs.

Saturday afternoon, in the midst of thronging crowds in town, I
saw a small, grubby-looking fox terrier sitting on the sidewalk, out
toward the edge of it but not out of reach of the traffic walking by.
Thoughtfully he was smelling every pair of legs that passed. He
would stretch his neck so as to start an exploration early, and his
nose would follow that pair of knees as long as he could reach them.
He was not worried or lost or anything of that sort. He was just
exploring, turning the pages of a book, and he was getting unmeasured interest out of it—manifestly so.

Farther along on the same busy sidewalk a large black dog stood
exactly in the middle of it, so that traffic parted and flowed by him
on either side. He also was giving close attention to passing legs,
first on one side and then on the other. He also was quite uncon-
cerned and was absorbed in what he was learning. Clearly each
passerby told him an extraordinary story which he could catch
instantly and then speculate on as long as the subject was in view.

Studious, inquiring, interested dogs! How I'd like to know what
they were discovering!

AN OMELET

The hour being late I decided to have an omelet. Three eggs, since there wouldn't be much else. I broke them into a bowl and beat them up, put a piece of butter in a small skillet and when it was properly hot poured in the frothy egg. Momentarily it all performed as it should. When it was far enough along I removed it to the oven to swell up before I folded it over.

But did it properly swell up? It did not. In the center it remained exactly as it was, but at the margin it rose and rose, up and up. When I looked into the oven it had the general appearance of an Indian basket—not quite so even along the edge or quite so symmetrical but unmistakably a basket. Considering the fact that it had accomplished this all by itself and in a dark oven and within three or four minutes it had done remarkably well.

I squashed one of its sides over upon the other, poured over it half a can of tomato soup, and ate it. But I think that I should have preserved it (it was really quite durable) and filled it with acorns or something and deposited it in the National Museum in the section devoted to ancient Hopi household utensils.

THE BASIC SUPPLY

This morning, as soon as I could distinguish the details of the sky, I found that a great, smooth mountain of soft, quiet gray filled all the space toward the east and southeast and all that across the south.

I think that it was the basic supply of gray, the general stock of reserves, we'll say, all waiting to be called upon for other mornings and, lot by lot, to be given special and particular shades and tints. I think that we can now be sure that there is a good supply on hand for the needs of weeks and months to come.

WHEN ANTLERS TOUCH

Let me tell you about a sound that I want to hear—

When caribou migrate, when their great herds converge, they rush along and forward together in a compact mass of great bodies. Then it is that their antlers touch, continuously touch, so that a characteristic sound is made as the many, broad antlers knock together.

It must be enchanting music as it drifts off on the swift keen wind of the Barren Lands!

ABSENT-MINDED

Is it an undesirable trait to be "absent-minded"? I wonder.

If the world that one can create out of one's own inner being is a vivid, absorbing world, why has it not the right to take precedence at times over the inconsequential physical world 'round about?

How can the inner world be all that it should be unless on occasion it can obliterate the outer? If the outer world breaks in upon it too easily, is the inner world as vivid as it should be?

I know that many persons "interrupt" easily. I mean that they are readily diverted from that which they happen to be doing. Those who are built that way may not have much patience with those who become deeply absorbed. The latter seem to them to be less than normally responsive, more than normally centered on a train of thought, "absent"-minded. But the truth seems to me to be that they are anything but *absent* minded!

FOOTSTEPS

Some day when I am but a lifeless thing
And crumble like a dead moth's wing,
Perhaps some free and formless inner gleam
Will rise from out the dust of my still heart
And with a swift and newborn will depart
In eagerness to far, ethereal lands.
Perhaps while there it will encounter bands
Of brave Cro-Magnons who will give
Mad tales of what it means to live
With meagre weapons where the mammoths roam,
And what it means to make a cave a home.
And then—and then—
Perhaps there'll be among those ancient men
Just one whose aged mem'ry can
Recall some legend of the Java Man!

FLORIDA

This morning, here in southern Florida, I have been driving since early hours through a tawny atmosphere—through smoke from one of the ground fires that seem always under way in this region, a tropically aromatic smoke from a pungent combination of fallen "fat pine" logs and dried palmetto leaves.

This same fat pine is burned in fireplaces here. Like other wood used in this area it is completely different from the fuel that occupies woodboxes in the North—different in appearance and different in performance.

The fat pine is rich in resin, so rich that sometimes it is translucent when you hold it up to the light. Often a log of it can be set afire with a single match. It is its own kindling and fuel, all in one. And the flame is very bright and luminous, like some broad and flaring torch.

But another aspect of it would not win it a place in a Northern woodshed. Every stick of it, or nearly every stick, has gone through at least one woods fire and has a generous black coating on at least one side. When you pick it up, seemingly that side is always underneath, lying in wait for you. And then it makes an all too abundant blackish or brownish smoke.

Oak is used along with the fat pine, to hold fire and to give it body and permanence. It is very solid and heavy oak, and it burns very slowly. The outside of a log takes on a soft, incandescent glow and remains that way while the log slowly diminishes in diameter.

I did not know that they use cypress also, but they do. Perhaps not much of it, for it cannot be as common and abundant as oak or pine. I was surprised to discover that cypress burns with a bright, fast flame. That doesn't seem appropriate for a tree that grows in swamps, that stands with its feet in water and carries festoons of Spanish moss on its branches. Cypress ought to be a wood that refuses to burn at all.

INDEPENDENCE

Across the aisle in the dining-car an elderly woman, well-dressed, pleasant, ample in build, determined. Evidently the car was a bit chilly for her. So she had procured from the waiter one of the car's gaily bordered lunch cloths, identical with those on the tables, and this she had drawn around her neck and shoulders as a scarf.

"Why not?" she seemed to say. "If you don't like it, go to thunder!"

Now I'll venture that not one woman in a thousand would dream of sitting there, placid and comfortable, with a dining-car lunch cloth for a temporary wrap. But I admired this lady for her originality and her independence.

SCULPTURED IN THE SAND

Your coming was a flooding touch,
A tidal wave upon my shore,
Engulfing all my life before
And leaving for all hours to come
A spindrift mist of magic lore.

You came, a fateful, chance-sent power,
And gave my soul—till then supine,
Till then inert, a mere outline,
A dim and planeless silhouette—
Dimensions, wide and deep and fine.

You've gone, and I'm alone once more,
In restless sleep upon my strand,
Where once your life-creating hand
Caressed the image of my soul
And left it sculptured in the sand.

Sweeps of gray clouds in the sky this afternoon, soft gray clouds that seemed to be silent and yet were saying, "Snow—snow!" A wind that had a moist cold breath in it, as if it had journeyed through a vast assembly of tiny ice crystals, all of which had imparted to it some bit of their own distinctive character. A wandering, lost snow-flake or two drifting down to earth—an outpost rider that had failed to note just when the host was scheduled to start and had got ahead of its companions, or maybe a hardy snow-flake soul that refused to wait for the rest.

What a long flight these frail, winged crystals make!—a mile, two miles—each drifting and descending along its own separate path. And each one different from any one of its neighbors, an individual with its own details of form and structure and adornment. Never among a thousand two precisely the same!

INFINITE

Do you like the word "infinite"? I often think of it. As a mere word it is ugly rather than beautiful or musical. But how completely mysterious in its descriptive meaning! It gives endlessness to time and space and distance. It carries thought of divinity to the ultimate. It gives limitless meaning to such qualities as power and mercy.

I like the word. I like to say it slowly and to use it rarely.

STARLINGS

I don't like them! And honestly they are the only birds about which I have that feeling.

When they perch in the top of a tree and utter their curious descending whistle it sounds ghoulish to me. When they fly I am critical of their too-short tails. When they walk they seem to have a graceless stride. Their beaks are too long and too yellow. And their eating habits are gluttonous, as if they were sure that they would be chased off in a moment, and meant to swallow everything possible in the brief time available.

No, I don't like them.

I think that there may be a reason for it that lies away back in mind and arises from that fact that they are undesirable importations, that they were brought over to this country by some misbeguided person who ought to have kept hands off our fauna. Also because they congregate in cities and like to make their nests in places and in ways that other and more attractive birds would not countenance. But even that doesn't seem to account sufficiently for my dislike. I must have been victim or enemy of starlings in some remote incarnation. A bird perhaps whose nest was robbed, or a berry too quickly swallowed.

I excuse other birds all sorts of things—willingly and gladly. Blue-jays are noisy and bold, but handsome and dashing. Chickadees are forever hungry, but sprightly and cheerful. Tree sparrows call each other names, but are interesting. Crows are loud and inclined to steal, but I respect their sagacity.

A starling is nothing that I like.

WORLD'S END

I want to be on a horse this morning, a horse with his head turned toward unmeasured spaces of wilderness, a quiet unambitious horse who doesn't care where he goes, or for how long he is gone. (Privately, he's *never* going to come back!)

Two or three pack-horses along—

Rain coming down softly on slickers—a soft gray sky—everlasting mountains—welcoming forests—hidden mountain meadows—clear streams—Thus for countless years on years!

Or—

A canoe, a good staunch, eighteen-foot canoe. Duffle in waterproof bags—raindrops dimpling the water—paddles moving smoothly—lake on lake—stream after stream—Thus to the very borders of the world!

GOING HOME

I have just watched a flock of gulls sail easily through the air, as though they were returning home from a hard day's labor. They flew slowly, lazily, wearily, calling out occasionally and, I thought, a bit complainingly. Definitely they were "going home."

HUMAN UNDERSTANDING

I am sure, very sure, that when we do not comprehend the act of another, the fault lies in our necessarily imperfect understanding.

We know so little, so very little, about the real inwardness of the individual human life—its vicissitudes and its secret aspirations, its failures and its successes, its yearnings, its sacrifices; so little about the manifold ways in which it fills or tries to fill its place among other lives.

Once in a while, once perhaps in a lifetime—for it can never happen except in marriage at its rare best or in an extraordinary friendship—we have a deep look within. When we do we see and comprehend.

Perhaps it is well that this is rare. Otherwise we should be totally overwhelmed by the extent, the intricacy, and the significance of what we beheld.

I wonder what the coal-mining country of the Pennsylvania Appalachians was like before the railroads came, and the lumbermen, and the miners. Don't you suppose that it may have been almost as beautiful as some of the foothill ranges of the West?

Whether the forests then had their areas of big evergreens I do not know. Probably they had. Certainly the oaks and maples and other hardwoods must have offered splendid, giant specimens. With woods everywhere I think that the streams must have been clear and sparkling.

The slopes and ridges and stone outcroppings are all there now for a setting. Looking upon them now, thinking of them as if clothed in continuous forest, forgetting the gashes made by railways, and the denuded hillsides where fire has burned away the earth, forgetting the soiled towns and the vast barren dumps from the outlets of coal mines, I can build in thought a rich region of varied and flowing beauty.

Perhaps if our civilization as it now exists retreats, one recompense will lie in the fact that healing natural forces will again come into their own. Squalid mining towns with their half-empty houses will disintegrate, and their decaying wood will become forest mold. Bushes will cover railway grades and coal dumps. The muddy waters in the rivers will again become clear. And wiser human beings, fewer in numbers, perhaps, will be glad for what sun and rain and earth set forth.

IF ONLY THE TIPS OF WINGS

Gentle World! Give me Peace today!
I need your cool kiss on my brow.
I need to have you tell me how
To live,
And how to harbor all you give.
I need the calmness of your plains,
The lullaby of soft-voiced rains,
The solace of a prairie breeze,
The soothing tune of aspen trees.
I need
To watch a downy, weightless seed
In lazy drift across my way,
To watch blue dragonflies at play,
And then to see a slim ant pass
Aslant a towering blade of grass.
I long
To greet some dainty bluet throng,
To kiss a willing violet,

33

To stroke a stalk of mignonette,
And then to lie within a glen
And hold communion with a wren.
I pray,
Tender World, let the timid wings
Of all these gentle things I seek
But brush their tips across my check.

CREDULITY

You know, there's a story, often repeated, that rats will carry eggs by using one rat as a sled. He lies on his back, so the yarn goes, and holds the egg with his legs. Other rats seize him by the tail and drag him. So!

But did you know that this story, in one form or another, goes back for hundreds of years? A German writer told it of marmots in a book published in the seventeenth century—how marmots carried their hay. Others about that time told it of badgers and of beavers. Sometimes the animal on its back was dragged by the tail, sometimes by other parts of its body. But the general proof was always the fact that animals were observed which did not have the normal amount of hair on their backs. Therefore, of course, it had been worn off by this dragging process.

But listen! The story dates further back than the seventeenth century. It goes clear back to Pliny.

Isn't it funny how a yarn such as that will live and be accepted, on and on, for hundreds of years!

APRIL STORM

A belated, out-of-season snowstorm continuously the last two days. It weighs down the branches, clings to every twig and pine needle, and obliterates every exposed square foot of ground that otherwise would be providing bits of provender for the small creatures who need it.

I wonder if such a storm does not come as a sad reversal of season in the lives of many wood folk.

Some of course are prepared. My chipmunk can again retire to his snug hole, wherever it is. I am certain that he has a pantry there that is thoroughly well stocked with the sunflower seeds and the cracked corn that he has been carrying off in his cheeks the last several days. The chickadees, too, cannot find the snow un-accustomed—and anyway they are too self-sufficient and well adapted to be distressed.

But the birds that have appeared since Winter undertook to depart—I wonder how they are faring. A bluebird in the midst of all this buried world! Those two robins who were fighting last week in the urge of Spring and the mating season! In the woods and fields there must be scores, hundreds, whose universe is suddenly upset. I shall be glad for them when it can be righted again.

35

The woods creatures—I said that they must feel the inversion of their world brought about by this great, thick, belated covering of snow.

The fact is intensely evident.

Last night in my driveway I surprised a pair of kildeer. Think of it!—those birds of summer meadows and pastures and the borders of streams and ponds. Now they found themselves in a snow-covered land. Since they do not perch on limbs (their toes are so arranged that perching is impossible), they had sought out this one bare bit of ground as a place to rest. One flew up from under my very feet. At the same moment another arose ahead, calling out the clear, ringing cry of its kind.

I found a mole, drowned or smothered in the heavy snow. The weather-turn was a catastrophe for him.

MODERN IMPROVEMENTS

I do not think that horses appreciate modern automatic wrapping machinery.

I saw a horse standing with his forefeet well up on the sidewalk. In front of him stood an old man. The man had two or three loaves of sugar, each nicely and securely done up in a well-pasted paper wrapper. He was trying to remove the wrapper from one of these and was having trouble with it. The more he tried the more the thing defied him and the more impatient the horse became. The man's hands fumbled and shook, and the horse's head went up and down.

From experiences of my own I sympathized with both the horse and the man. I have felt like both.

A WISH

I long to search and find in space
The faintest, briefest, vaguest trace
Of thought waves as they travel by.
I long to touch one curving line
And make that thought wave wholly mine.
I long to hold it in my hand,
To see—to understand.

BOYS

Speaking of cold days: on the fifth of April (I noted the date and remember it) about five o'clock in the evening I was driving. I looked off over the marshes with their deep-banked creeks. The air was cold and damp. I saw a fire—high flames and a great deal of smoke. It was built on the edge of the creek against the damp bank. Around the fire were gathered about eight boys. I should say that they were about ten or eleven years old. Three of them— one sitting on a high, upturned crate, another hopping from one foot to the other, and the third standing still—were totally without clothes. I laughed and laughed. You must remember it was a cold, damp, early April day and the sun was fast setting.

The other boys were on their way to total nudity and I saw a glorious assortment of drawers. One boy was burdened with *red* drawers—yes *red*—and I assume they were flannel.

Will you please tell me why they picked such a day and hour for such an assembly? Of course they were warm in front, but their very definite backs must have been cold indeed. I wish that I might have asked them "Why?" Perhaps they had all fallen into the creek and were taking this painful method of drying out. Perhaps it was a secret society. Perhaps it was a nudist colony.

I love boys, love their unexpected, particular, individual brand of insanity. I am always glad to come upon a bit of absorption like this.

WANDERINGS

Last night I slept very little and found myself reading at three and four o'clock in the morning. In those wakeful small hours I heard rain falling in a melodious patter upon a roof-top outside my window.

As I listened I heard rain in Colorado on the skree slopes—I heard rain in Montana making soft mud under my horse's hoofs— I heard rain in the bush in the far North falling upon bright red pigeon berries—I heard it again in the Gaspé, in our own nearby woods, in every place where I had heard it with pleasure before.

In those minutes of conscious listening there came to me a sense of physical ease that I have not felt for weeks.

THE TURN OF THE WHEEL

Sometime I want to sit down and write about the turn of the wheel that may tear a human being loose from all ordinary and accustomed pursuits and cast him bodily into activities that presently turn out to be the life that he *should* have been leading. I want to write about the trick of fate (unkind it may have seemed at the time—illness, loss of position, dire necessity) that may make a human being find himself in spite of himself; about the rare, the very rare person who dares to break away from the habitual and to substitute for the wearing round of "holding down a job" the one pursuit that in the back of his mind he is forever wishing to follow.

I am quite certain that sometimes only a violent upheaval can open the way, that in the lives of those men and women who accomplish that which is genuinely outstanding there may be, in some instances at least, a great denial of that which holds the rest of us bound.

IRELAND

I have been reading Irish tales. But the reading has not been continuous. I have been looking into the fire and remembering— seeing once more the lovely town of Adare, cloud-shadowed Kenmare Bay, and the hills of Connemara. I've been watching jackdaws on the roof-tops of the gray stone houses of Galway, williewagtails and corncrakes sweeping across the road. I've been enjoying the tumult of the cattle-and-sheep fairs and the glamour of Dublin at night. I've been remembering the growing things of Ireland—heather, broom, fuschias in profusion, and flowers, large ferns, and green moss—all that have roots in Irish soil and welcome Irish rains.

It is good to have the power to remember.

HARBOR DREAMS

When the soft-voiced water gleams
As the moonlight sends soft dreams
To the harbor's quiet breast,
Then the night breeze whispers "Rest!"
To the vessel coming home
With its trail of tired foam.
Dusky shadows softly creep
Lulling each dim boat to sleep
As it leans against its pier,
Safe from wind and wave-born fear.
All the outlined tall mast tips
And the caverned ferry slips,
All the waiting hills of coal,
Form a blended soft-stroked whole,
As all harmony of line
Flows to form the hushed design.
Not a gull is seen to ride
With the motion of the tide,
Not a winch is heard to creak,
Not a ghost is heard to speak.
All is silent, calm, and still,
All will slumber on until
Each bright riding light grows pale
And a new-born dawn sets sail.

Every few yards in my woods this week I come upon lady-slipper orchids—luxuriant, fresh, in the height of color and stature. Some of them are a rich, deep red.

I rather like the other name for them—"moccasin flower." That vestibule that the bumble-bee enters is well patterned after the toe of an Indian moccasin—and I like to think of moccasins rather than lady's slippers.

A WORLD APART

We human beings are accustomed to thinking of our towns and highways as the centers of all activity—centers surrounded by a sort of unimportant, green vegetative border of fields and woods.

Yet everywhere in those woods and fields there are centers of equally animated activity—intimate, purposeful life—and to those centers the highways and towns and all that they represent are only the border, the negligible, necessary border.

This afternoon I went to the shaggy opening in my woods where a flicker has a new nest in an old tree, and lay down to watch the hole leading into this house.

All the time that I was there I was in a world set apart from the surrounding regions. From the highway beyond the woods came a continuous hum and roar of motor cars. It seemed that there was never a moment when I could not hear them. Once there was the distant clatter and louder roar of a passing train. But in the opening in the woods all was different. A spider was spinning a web near my head. Ants were busy about their affairs.

CLOISTERED

Ah! look within my soul and see
Rare love and all humility,
Both buried there
For you to find
When you alone unlock my mind.

My words are false that make you feel
My heart is but a myth, unreal.
It lives apart
And bides the day
When you alone will find the way.

Ah! Love, draw near the bastioned wall.
Fear not! It only waits to fall.
Love, come to me
And I shall show
To you alone the inner glow!

RED-WINGED BLACKBIRDS

This morning outside my cabin an unexpected flock of birds that must have arrived after a sky journey—a whole throng of red-winged blackbirds. I heard them before I got up. Presently they were under my windows and the air was full of their cheery, reedy call. Their epaulets were quite rusty, showing no scarlet and orange at all but only faded and tarnished yellow. They have not yet acquired their new uniforms—though I suspect that they have been measured for them and that initial work on them is started. But their voices are as always.

HUSBANDRY

All day I have been banging back and forth like a bell-clapper—this and that and the other job in succession. Now I propose to think of something else, and my inclination is toward the frivolous and uncomplicated and even simple-minded—not just simple but simple-minded.

You'll laugh when I tell you that I carry with me as the uppermost thought in my mind at the moment a smell—just that, a smell—that I encountered on my way past a college field as I was going to the railway station a few minutes ago. It was such an uncollegiate smell, an unacademic odor, a thing not of cloisters and ivied walls, an uneducated, unrefined, unmitigated aroma. It made me think a whole train of thoughts having to do with the aspects of husbandry, with the nice names that folk try to use for the article in question, and my reaction when I hear the nice names used.

They have been heaping this pile in the field for a number of days or weeks. They haul out loads and add them to the accumulation, and they send out wagon-like contrivances on which they load portions of the heap and then drive across the field with a great clatter and a flying curtain of small particles at the rear, and an aura all about—front, sides, and rear.

Every once in a while I hear some old lady or some white-haired gentleman speak of a pile like that as "dressing." I never can become reconciled to the designation. On the one hand it suggests connotations in the way of sterile gauze and iodine and such like—violently out of place in this instance—and on the other I think of French and Russian and lettuce and so on—and that doesn't help either.

Of course the whole thing is a sort of temporary monument to the continuing usefulness of the horse. One ought not to complain.

AUSTRALIAN PINE

Do you know about the Australian Pine? Not a pine-tree at all, or even an evergreen, but with every characteristic such as to make it appear to be a pine. Needles that are actually twigs. Leaves reduced to tiny scales. A seed cluster that looks like a cone. Yet the tree is a dicotyledon, in the same great botanical group as our maples and oaks and elms.

GOSSAMER

Life offers at times such brief, gossamer hours that when they are gone there seems to be a minor song in the air, soft, more distant all the time, and yet in some way touched with immortality.

MATING

The blossoms of flowers—what a lovely thing they make of the spirit of mating, of bringing a new generation into existence! It seems to me that their ways are a symbol of the inner rightness, the essential nobility and beauty, of union.

The petal from an apple blossom drifting into my car—satiny, delicate of tint, a bit of the housing for the quiet, thrilling drama that has been played on the tip of a twig in preparation for new life! The apple blossoms were not hidden, not concealed as something sordid or shameful. They were the consummation of glory and fulfillment.

THE SHOWER

Dawn—a bird—and a meadow—
Dew and a Grail-like flower—
Flight and its feathered shadow—
Merged by some mystic power!
Rest—a stalk that is fragile—
Dew and a trembling flower—
Flight that is careless—agile—
Birth of a tiny shower!

MAHLER

A glorious orchestra tonight! Throughout the playing of Mahler's First Symphony in D major I listened with a growing desire for something that could never be. I wanted to hear it all again played out-of-doors—in a soft woods of gentle trees. I wanted to lie on the ground with my eyes closed and listen. I wanted to hear the sound of a summer breeze in leafed trees blend with the music as Mahler wrote it. I wanted all this knowing that it could never be. And so with my joy there was a touch of sadness. And then I found in the music the same touch of sadness that was within me.

A rare hour of response! Would that the dead composer might know that the message of his music reached a depth within me.

SAGE

My train was crossing Wyoming. Through the open window came an unmistakable, pungent, wild, lovely odor—the aroma of sage. A shower had set free its fragrance, I think. Of all the plants of this region this is perhaps the one that most vividly brings to the visitor, through its odor, the spirit of the vast, rolling, open spaces of the foothills bordering the Rockies. It has a way all its own and it is the essence of the region.

DESPOILED

If I were a tree in a city park, or on a university campus, or in some one's elaborate estate, I'd feel embarrassed to have the ground around my feet treated as I have seen it treated.

Today I walked through a park. Beneath a group of pine trees the ground was raked completely bare. Not one glowing brown needle remained—nothing but the marks of iron rake teeth in the hard, naked soil. Beneath maples and other hardwoods there was closely clipped grass, as tightly clipped as the head of a convict. And worst of all, around the foot of each tree a small, neat, exact circle of spaded earth, a little circle about two or three feet in diameter.

I felt as if the pine trees had been robbed—and as for the maples I had the feeling that they were like mature, grownup creatures that had been dishonored.

BELLS

I have been reading about bells—and it is a most surprising subject, with all manner of historic lore and legend tied up in it. I have only made a start.

Did you know that bells are not definitely known to have existed earlier than the beginning of the Christian era—not even in China —and that our present form of bell did not evolve before the year 1500? Prior to that time bells were different in shape and proportions from what they are now, and still earlier they were made of plates fastened together in a sort of rectangular shape.

One of the earliest references to bells is to be found in Irish records dating about 500 A. D. (In Belfast today there is an ancient bell, decorated, set with jewels, believed to be referred to in these documents.) And that is as early as any similar records go in old Rome.

And do you know that a bell really has five notes, not just one? If it is a good bell, properly tuned, all five will be in the right relationship, and such a bell will have a pleasing quality not otherwise found. Few bells, until somewhat recent years, have been so tuned as to have all these notes right. Most were made in such form that they were out of *real* tune. They were filed and worked over only to the extent of getting one note at the right pitch—perhaps the "strike" note, or maybe the "hum" note (which is a major 6th lower).

To bell men and bell ringers a bell is always "she," never "it." And the biggest bell in a ring is always the "tenor," never the "bass."

When it comes to "change-ringing" (the ringing of the bells of a set in a series of varied sequences), the subject becomes extensive and complicated. There are many historic systems of change-ringing. Some of these are identified by names and have been well known for many generations. The possible combinations, even with a ring of twelve bells, are almost endless—and that, apparently, is the origin of the expression "ringing the changes."

It's all tied up with men's customs and history.

NIGHTTIME

There's terror in the Night
For folks who are like me,
For goblins, ghosts, and witches
Are lurking near each tree.

My friends will not believe
A single word I say,
Especially that *once*
A monster barred my way.

Of course it's very hard
To find beneath your feet
A dinosaur in search
Of dainty things to eat.

But worst of all to me,
A thing that makes me quail,
Is just a large-eyed mouse
That trails a long, thin tail!

FIREFLIES

I wonder how far the light of a firefly can be seen by other fireflies. I wonder what it looks like to them—what inner glows it arouses within the body of those who catch its gleam.

We know that the character of the light varies among different species for it is a selective attraction between the sexes. The fireflies of a given species respond only to the light that characterizes their kind. We know that the light itself, not some other emanation, attracts, for females in a bottle brought males to them by their flashes, while females in a perforated cylinder that obscured the light were unable to attract their mates.

Fireflies feed on other small living creatures. I wonder if these others recognize the imminent danger in the flashing light and shrink from its approach, now visible, now ominously quenched.

"CONFERENCES"

Is there anything in the world that is more wearing, more racking, more penetratingly and cumulatively painful, than sitting at a conference or committee meeting that moves like winter molasses?

Today I have so sat. I sat until I creaked when I moved, until I grew fast to my chair, or would have if I hadn't squirmed and twisted and jiggled and fidgeted. I sat until mentally I was like a mixture of some animal in a stupor combined with an entirely different animal that was about to bite the first creature within reach. Finally, though some stolid persons stayed, unmoved and undisturbed, I ran away and caught a train this afternoon instead of waiting until the sleeper. The rest could stay and finish and be hanged for all I cared.

AT ONE'S BIDDING

When a trying day's work is ended, how swiftly it can all be banished just by summoning other things to mind!

A moment ago came at my bidding:

A sunset sky behind snowy peaks in the Rockies—

Fields of grain bending before the wind—

Quiet aisles in deep woods—

A little wilderness lake, its water motionless, its trees standing silent around its border—

The long, long sweep of a deserted sand beach, with great slow waves from the vast Pacific falling majestically upon its margin—

Aspen leaves fluttering in the morning sunlight—

Glowing coals beneath a camp-fire—

Little ripples lapping against a canoe—

Moist gray mist, and round crystal droplets clinging to leaves—

And so on and on—

THE SCHEME OF THINGS

On a country road I saw a young hawk sitting on a bleached gray tree-trunk. In the sunlight he blended with his pedestal and in his immobility looked like a carving of great perfection. A breeze ruffled his breast feathers. He bent his head to one side. He saw me. And at last in leisurely fashion he spread his fine wings and flew away. I tried hard to think of his predatory habits, tried to feel that he was a knave, but I could not. He remained to me simply a beautiful living creature that belonged in the scheme of things, even as I.

GRASS

Great areas of soft, gray-yellow grass in the open spaces of this mid-West country through which my train is passing. All of it, every spear, bends toward the east—silent witness to the high winds of the last few days that have swept this region and have made all these tiny stems incline their bodies before it. All of them seemingly are alike in their curves away from the west. All appear to be alike in form and structure and color. Yet every least one of the myriad host is an individual, with its own characteristics, its own shape and detail of leaf, its own delicate tint, its own minute pattern of raceme.

We speak of "species" as if a million plants, such as a million grass plants, were precisely identical, exactly the same, like coins. To do this is convenient and necessary for the classifier. He points to broad facts, such as the usual length of stem, the typical shape of leaf, the characteristic arrangement of flowers. Yet each is different from all others. If one could search long enough one might find an individual that lay out toward the border of the "usual characteristics," approaching in details another individual of another closely related species, also out toward the border of that species. One might find no gulf separating these two, but rather almost a merging of the one into the other.

Science is not exact. It approximates. There is no absolute uniformity anywhere whatever in all the world. Atoms and molecules may be individualistic. The fact that they are too small for us to see them does not necessarily mean that they are identical.

Would it not be enlightening if we could see and feel and hear the utterly minute differences that must exist everywhere among all things—could see how the least part of the smallest flower differs from all its companions, how even a steel ball is different from all other steel balls!

And human beings! Think in what myriad ways each differs from all others! Yet governments are set up and laws are enacted and social rules are crystallized and enforced as if millions were quite alike. Is it any wonder that in the enforced adherence to multiple regulations in present-day life—in standardized school programs, standardized jobs, standardized housing, standardized laws and all else—is it any wonder that there are millions of misfits among the hundreds of millions of persons in the civilized world?

BY THE RUNNING TIDE

I would go where periwinkles press
Their moist and open-lipped caress
Upon a beach beneath a surf-worn crag.
I would watch the ribboned seaweeds lag
In limp and purple dampness, touched with foam,
When white-tipped waves set forth for home.
I would be a shadow on that strand,
As silent as the silver sand,
And I would seek the deep-sea sprites that hide
In all the hollows of the running tide!

MARIGOLDS

Tonight I spent a few moments in my blossoming garden. I arranged some marigolds that were walking on one another's toes. Their slender, thread-like roots were all ensnarled.

I like the fragrance of marigolds. It is earth-like. It seems to be taken from the soil itself, up through the stem and out to the leaves and blossoms. I like to touch them and to have the fragrance linger on my finger tips. Their aroma comes right from the heart of the marigold. It is no surface sweetness.

Marigolds! Yes, I too like their individualistic odor. It is a sort of unsocial fragrance—no ordinary drawing-room sweetness, no delicate hothouse scent, but a downright marigold fragrance, honest, direct, pungent, provocative, almost pugnacious, and certainly standing on its own good rights.

HEAT

Last night in this crowded city I wanted personally to help the sun to set. I wanted to lean over the edge of the earth, put my hand upon the sun, and push it far, far away. I should not have cared if the earth swung forever from its orbit and no longer travelled with the sun. I should not have cared if a chill came upon the earth, then frost, then ice, then a permanent ice-cap. I should not have cared if all living creatures were in this way obliterated.

I can not imagine why tribes in the past indulged in sun worship.

POND EVENING

It was raining quietly when I visited my pond at dusk one night this week. Standing very still I could hear the drops ring as they struck the water. They made a sound like that of a tiny brook flowing in the midst of clean stones and dropping over tiny waterfalls. It was a dainty, beautiful bit of music. Back of it and beneath it was a soft murmuring rustle as the rain found its way down through the leaves and the pine needles of the woods bordering the pond. Some of the raindrops made clear bubbles as they struck the surface of the pond—evanescent little half-globes that floated for a moment and then vanished.

As I stood near the bank a muskrat suddenly appeared, almost beneath my feet. He had come up from some affair under water. He did not see me, but went swimming steadily away, his submerged legs and tail making little swirling eddies, his dark head moving steadily along. On and on he went, to some upper reach of the pond—to his home in a bank somewhere, I suspect—probably to his waiting mate and children.

IT DOES NOT WEEP

Why must the weeping willow
Symbolize unending sleep?
It does not weep!
Why must it seem to droop
Above the tender grass?
I know it does but stoop
To touch all those who pass.
I've seen the weeping willow
Swaying,
Playing,
When each soft Summer breeze
Hummed music for the lush-leafed trees.
Ah!, then it was not sad,
Remindful of the tomb,
But all abandon, mad,
Without a thought of doom.
I've seen the weeping willow
Basking,
Asking
The breath of early Spring
For all that life can bring.
I've seen it bend above the deep,
Swift waters of a stream,
And then it did not weep—
It did but wait—and dream!

ORIOLE

The oriole!

Is it not impressive to think how these chaps have come all the way from the tropics—maybe even from the upper Amazon or the Orinoco—flying over all those thousands of miles of forests and fields and jungle! What a journey!

HUMANITY

Coming across New York I walked along east 14th Street, looking at humanity—sheer, crowding humanity.

The sidewalk lined with peddlers and their stocks. Suspenders, hanging from a wooden bar, carried by a voluble man, minus coat and vest, who continually stretched one out and let it snap back, over and over. Ice cream rolls, the vendor cutting off a slice while you wait. Razor blades in little packages, all in rows in a little box held against the man's stomach by a strap over his shoulders. Strips of cocoanut meat, cut from the parent nut and now being sprinkled with a watering can to keep them fresh—and on the same push-wagon a white-painted keg containing cocoanut milk, five cents a glass. Push-carts of grapes, big, red, California grapes.

A large, hot, noisy arcade, filled with a throng of men, women, boys, girls, all eating hot dogs and sandwiches, and drinking sodas and beer. Men selling lurid song-sheets. A drunk squaring himself away for his uncertain voyage through the midst of the people. Small boys, a group of them, each equipped with a stock of half-a-dozen large manila bags with cord handles, to peddle to shoppers, but all engaged in a sidewalk game and forgetting to sell their merchandise. Humanity! Crowding, hurrying humanity!

HARVEST

About six this morning there was a tapping on the screen wire, here and there, near my bunk on my cabin porch. Sometimes the tapping became a vigorous whack. It waked me up. As I looked I saw that a bird was collecting flies and small moths from the screen. I'd had my light on while reading last night, and of course various bugs had flown to the screen and were still there this morning. The bird seemed to be one of the flycatcher tribe, but I do not know which one.

NORTHERN ONTARIO

I have been journeying through the wilderness of northern Ontario.

It was only yesterday, I am sure, that the great ice-cap receded from this remote area. All these lonely lakes seem so fresh, so filled with clear, cool water, so virgin as to shore line, as yet so unreached by human beings. There are hundreds upon hundreds of these lakes, varying as to contours and island content, but all with the same fundamental characteristic silence.

As I passed each lake I longed to be in moccasins and standing there on the shore—standing quietly on a rock, looking into the water and listening to the lap of the tiny waves—or plodding through the muskeg.

THROUGH THE PINES

A million silken tunes all merge
To make the volumed sound
That falls and rises like the surge
Of waves on tide-washed ground.

A million silken tunes that run
A swift, crescendoed race.
Soft music, only now begun,
Now fading off in space.

Dim notes in oft repeated theme,
The song of wind and tree,
The restless surge and lull that seem
In kinship with the sea!

EARLY HOURS

I wish that it were possible to change completely the customary hours and circumstances for some ordinary human activities. Hours for meals and for sleep, for example.

Take sleep. There is only one right place for a bed, and that is as nearly in the open as it can be arranged. It *ought* to be under the sky, or just beneath the shelter of trees. I think that going into a dark room to sleep, away from windows, shut off from the freedom of the clean outdoors, is as if some creature that belongs in the treetops were to descend into a burrow in the ground.

If it can have its opportunity the growing daylight, stealing through eyelids, says "Behold! Another day! A thousand new adventures await!" Folk in houses, in darkened rooms, can not hear and appreciate the call. They have not learned about the rare quality of early morning sun and flowing air, all fresh and alert after the dark night.

So it is, then, that we have "Breakfast at eight," or later. The waste of it! I should like to breakfast many times each year by candlelight—or at least to be up and out with the dawn. Lunch, then, at an hour that is rightly adjusted to all this, and an evening meal early because it should not interfere with seeing sunsets or listening to evening birdnotes or watching stars come out.

Of course it's all impossible. It doesn't fit in. But it seems to me that being a part of a complex social, business, and professional existence makes many good things impossible.

RAINBOW

Driving today through rain I came out of the shower and into bright, gay sunlight. The air was washed sparkingly clean, and all the trees and bushes and meadows were vivid in their freshly laundered dress.

Presently I saw a segment of rainbow ahead of me—and I am child or primitive, or savage, enough always to feel an uplift when I see a rainbow. Its promise to me is real and full of portent. After a time there were tiny, misty droplets on my windshield, and by that I knew that I was driving through the rainbow itself. So I think that I must have absorbed its promise to the full.

TUMBLE-WEED

Returning through the West I saw a great company of remarkable travellers. All along the wire fence bordering the railroad right-of-way lay a windrow of tumble-weed. Extraordinary wanderers! A whole section of a plant, or its whole body, permitting itself to be detached from the roots and giving itself up to the wind, that it may roll over and over and thus achieve a new place for tumble-weed to grow.

THIS DELICATELY POISED WORLD

What an intricate and delicately poised world we have all about us! How remarkably and completely the parts fit into one another!

In front of my cabin there is an old apple-tree, with a big hollow and dead limbs. A chipmunk lives there. Under it a fallen limb encourages the grass to grow high. Beyond it there is a dense clump of tall weeds and bushes. Birds sing from its shelter. Near by another thicket extends as far as the margin of the woods. Burdocks cover the ground there, and above these rise tall elderberries. Beneath the burdocks small rabbits play, and in the elderberries a shy catbird found concealment for her nest.

Everywhere an intricate pattern of adjustment! Each part suited in its own way to the needs of those who live there. What would the chipmunk do without the hollow into which to dodge when the chickadees attempt to assault him—and how could the young child of the vigorous chickadee learn what to do without the combination of twigs, hollow, parent, and chipmunk?

No humanly preordered and prearranged system is this! Things happen as they should and as they have happened since time began, and talents are developed and quickened in proportionate degree. Fill up the hollow trunk of the tree, cut the weeds, trim the bushes, and life might thus be made smoother and safer for the chickadee youngster—but in the end there would be only a dependent adult bird instead of a normal one—if indeed the youngster ever became an adult at all.

TWILIGHT

Twilight—
Valley that lies between
The stark, bright light
Of day and the soft-toned sheen
Of night,
You hold in your hollowed heart
Myriad views and sounds,
The lure of lower grounds.

Twilight—
Keeper of rainbow clouds
And silent crowds
Of fireflies that light the fields.
Hushed time,
When clear on your scented air
Notes of a resting bird
In vibrant tones are heard.

Twilight—
End of the seething day
That flows away,
Soft prelude to rising night.
Gray time,
Shadowed by higher peaks,
Yours is a valley's calm
Where panting hours disarm!

There is a beautiful garden now beside the wood-road that leads to my cabin. As you enter it you find tall meadowsweet and steeplebush, white and faintly pink and deep rose. Across from these a thick tangle of blackberries, and a clinging vine with the tiniest of four-petaled white flowers. Farther along a border of goldenrod. And still farther a tall, luxuriant forest of ferns. A rich and beautiful garden, planted by the wind and by bees, and watered by showers.

DANCE!

Tall weeds that bend above a stream,
Tossing seeds upon its breast,
Sending shadows where some gleam
Of tawny sunlight seeks to rest,
Dance! With all the stepless grace
Of temple maidens who adore
Gods of full and wondrous life,
Touch thy garments to the shore!
Hear the music of the breeze
That sweeps and drifts like some vague dream
Around thy form and through the trees
And plays a largo with the stream!

ROBINS

I think that the robin definitely has earned his prominent place in the world, and I am certain that he is entitled to his rotund figure.

Always, invariably, he is the first creature up in the morning. He sings to the dawn before the sun has even begun to approach the morning horizon. He is eternally busy all day, except when he takes his post in a treetop and chants a hundred bars or so of his devotedly favorite song. He searches for worms until the very last trace of daylight. He is capable of even more than that. Last night, after it was quite dark, I walked across the park, and Behold!, there were two robins hopping about where electric lights shone on the grass, still looking for worms. Every other bird whatever had gone to bed and to sleep. But not the robin.

He is broad in his tolerance as to nesting place and he wastes no time on concealment. On a beam in my carriage house there are four robin's nests in a row, touching one another, like four apartments on a city street. I almost expect to see a number plate on each, and to find that a robin carries a latchkey and has a telephone number in a book.

INSECT MUSIC

Several times lately, in reading, I have encountered comments on the Orientals' (Chinese and Japanese) love of insect music—comments deploring the indifference of our Western world to these sweet sounds. The music of the cricket, for example.

Always I have loved the sounds made by insects, their whirring and humming and buzzing and chirping. I have felt this to be the most mysterious, the most hidden, the most elusive of natural music. I have stretched out in dried grass for hours in Summer with my head on my arms and listened and listened.

THE PROSPECTOR

With your overladen pack
You're starting on your way,
And you'll not be coming back
For two years and a day.

So you're going to seek for gold!
You've mapped out all your trail.
How I wish I could be told
Your searching will not fail!

Ah, Good-bye!, my Passerby,
And Thanks!, for don't you see,
All the high hope in your eye
Has entered into me!

YOUTH

This week I talked to a class of University students. With every such group that I meet I find myself wishing, wishing, that some spark could set alight in them an eagerness of mind, an awakened imagination, a sort of divine mental activity that would lead them to seek, to be aware, to reach out and grasp new thoughts and facts and impressions, to look for the hidden cause and relationship, to realize that in the world immediately about them, within touch of their fingers, there is mystery and romance awaiting their finding. They seem to expect only dead and dried facts, long since assorted and classified. That everything is not already discovered and determined and certified seems not to have occurred to most of them.

I would rather that they themselves make one little discovery of their own, out of their own initiative, and thus learn that they have powers that are only waiting to be utilized, than that they memorize all the facts in someone's book. I would rather that they summon one glowing vision out of their own quickened imagination than that they learn a thousand formulae and rules.

There are courses that universities do not give that I believe would be challenging and productive.

One of these would be training in imagination. I think that it *can* be trained and quickened and given its right significance, so that it may become the productive power that it should be, and that it may become the joy to its possessor that it ought to be.

And another would be training in observation, in the alert use of all the human senses, in seeing and hearing and feeling what can never be perceived except by the eager, searching eye and ear and touch. I am certain that the world 'round about could be made immeasurably richer. And I am certain that as responsiveness increased, receptiveness and retentiveness would grow also.

FLIGHT

Mist defined the winding upper part of my pond tonight, not lying upon the water but poised a little way above it. And overhead were swifts, wheeling, gliding, turning sharply, beating the air with rapid wings at times in their tireless and beautifully skilful quest for their evening meal. Sometimes one of them would coast for two or three seconds with wings almost closed against its body—an ultra-rapid bit of motion through the air, almost like that of a projectile.

CROW INDIAN

A beautiful Indian book, "Red Mother," a story told (in sign language and by interpreter) by an aged Crow squaw of Montana . . . .

Again that beautiful everyday imagery of the vanishing Indian! Pemmican is spoken about. There is reference to habits and possessions that are strange to us: the bleached shoulder bone of a buffalo for one's plate—a cloth beneath of rawhide—a mountain sheep's horn for one's cup—buffalo hides upon which to sleep—all within a tepee. (I seem to be there while I read.) One child in the book had a treasured toy, the membrane from the heart of a buffalo, stuffed with hair until it was a ball, then the outside painted blue and red.

A pity that we cannot fashion, ourselves, the toys that we give! Then it would not be the child alone that received joy from them.

GASPE

For several days I have been sharing in the life of a Gaspe road. It is absorbing.

Up and down my road, day in and day out, early and late, goes a procession of tin pails, each bearing a monogram in bright red letters. Once they held lard. Now they serve a universal use as the means of carrying anything and everything, from groceries to water.

They are of various sizes, from little pails holding a quart or two up to big ones with a capacity of two or three gallons. No doubt the origin of the variation lies far back in the number of pennies or of big Canadian paper dollars that the family chanced to possess at the moment, or the stock of merchandise that the village store had on its shelves. In any case the outcome is a container that conveniently varies with the volume of contents to be transported, and with the size and age of the person doing the transporting. But always the red monogram!

I think that there must be a certain fine contentment, a certain inner satisfaction, in thus acquiring, as a sort of by-product, an article of such adaptability and such daily use. Even while the shortening that comes in the pail is serving its purpose there must lie in the background of thought the fact that another handy household adjunct, a bright new one, is waiting to begin its useful life.

THE MEETING

I watched the rays that lingered when the sun had set
Touch with loving light, as if they longed to stay,
The scarlet trees that tipped a rounded hill.
I watched with breath so still
The lonely silence paid no heed to me.
Soon the passion of those rays grew so intense
That twilight felt the throbbing pain of sweet suspense.
Then Lo!, without timidity or shame,
Those virgin woods that graced the hill above
Surrendered all their beauty to the touch of Love.

REMARKS AND ASIDES

Today an occasional soft, busy note of a bird reaches me—not the outpourings of sunrise but the little remarks and asides of birds that are busy with the day's undertakings.

Always there is a thrill in the spontaneous carols that come pouring from the throats of birds at the earliest light of a new day, and equally in the sustained song with which some birds gesture in sound to the setting sun. But I like also the half-unconscious notes that come from them as they fill the hours between with their duties.

SQUIRRELS

The squirrels around my cabin are an unfailing source of interest. Early this morning one bounced down upon my roof. I looked out of the front door. At that moment he arrived on a rafter of my new porch, a few feet from me. He stopped instantly, and we both stood there motionless, eyeing each other. This performance lasted until I got tired of it. I gave a sudden jerk and jump. He did likewise, but stood his ground. I repeated it, with the same result. Finally I retreated, whereupon he went along to the tree that no doubt he was bound for.

CONTRAST

As I walked along a country road last week, familiar but un-visited for a time, I found that farm-hands had cleared the roadside next to a cultivated field. Weeds and grasses had been mowed clean, bushes cut level with the ground, the low limbs of trees removed. Good husbandry no doubt! But where a gay company of daisies and fire-weed had been, now only heaps of brown stalks remained.

On the opposite side the road borders an old pasture that has not fallen into the maw of civilization's needs. Here the variegated and absorbing company remained unharmed. Junipers still crowded over the stone wall, birches sent their sprouts out to assault the road's border, meadowsweet and steeple-bush lifted their flower spikes above the tangle. Here young rabbits have their retreat. I am glad that their home has chanced to be on the right side of the road.

The contrast! On one side a mowed border, a wire fence, and behind it cattle—useful brutes, no doubt. On the other side a great community of weeds, junipers, birches, and pines, in the midst of which dwell rabbits and woodchucks, thrushes and warblers—useless creatures, perhaps!

I presume that we must have both sides.

SISAL

The sisal plant, and its neat arrangement for the future! I have run across it in a visit to the Tropics and I have found it most interesting. (This is the plant, you know, from the leaves of which fibres are obtained for making rope.)

Up from the heart of the plant grows a great, tall flowerstock, twelve or fifteen feet high, with wide-spreading branches. Out on these branches, well away from the central stalk, clusters of flowers develop. In time each cluster comes to possess all the essentials of a new sisal plant, including a mass of bare, waiting roots. Then when all is complete and ready, a cluster lets go and falls to the ground. Forthwith the roots take hold, the flow of soil moisture to the small stalk and leaves begins, and a new and independent sisal has started on its career.

SINGING ALONE

Today in driving I found a cross-road through farm country. I drove so slowly that I could see things that were growing by the road and see little birds here and there. To be sure, my road ended in rocks and dust and bumps, but I had it to myself the entire way.

If you will tell no one on earth I shall tell you that I sang aloud on the lonely road. I, like the toad, am supposed to have no singing voice at all. But anyway it was a lonely road, and even if the notes were wrong the spirit of the song was there.

DEFENSES

What a continuous, unremitting series of impacts, a human being must meet each day! Every hour, every instant, his surroundings crowd upon his senses. Whether he wishes it or not, his eyes must see and must transmit to his mind a thousand impressions, moment by moment, during all of the time that he is awake. His ears and other senses add to the total. Everything that comes near to him asks for entry—every person, every possible source of contact and impact, large and small, pleasant and unpleasant, helpful and harmful, significant and transitory.

We speak often of conserving our output of energy, but I think that it may be equally important to preserve and to build up our defenses against the rush of our surroundings. I think that we can, in a measure, control the access to our inner being, that we can consciously select what we shall fully respond to and what we shall let pass. I believe that it may be greatly worth while to do this.

We see and hear and feel most clearly that which has had a place prepared for it already in our mind. If I would be completely aware of an elusive song of a bird I must be receptive to bird songs. If I think of them, listen for them, consider their tone and quality and sequence when I chance to hear them, I shall become receptive to them and I shall hear them when otherwise they would not reach my consciousness. If I would really see the colors in field and sky, I shall the better attain that responsiveness if I *think* of and look for the colors in everything around me. If I would see and understand the human story in the faces of those whom I meet, I must remember always what stories a human face can tell.

But if I listen consciously to the din of modern, mechanized existence, I shall become the more sensitive to sounds of that nature. If I think constantly of the discords of human quarrels, I shall hear more and more those symbols of human misunderstandings. If I seek perplexities and distractions I shall find them.

I am sure that human beings have the power to choose—not completely, not always, not with invariable satisfaction—but still to choose. And I am sure that in the thoughtful exercise of that power human life can be enriched.

ONE WISH

Let me lie upon an open, sloping hill.
Let all the world be dark and still.
Bid the full moon mount the sky.
And then, as there I lie,
Let the swift and southward flight
Of geese that migrate through the night
Cross before the moon's clear face.
Let me see their wild and shadowed grace.

SWIFT WINDS

One must notice the wind today—it blows so strongly. I like it
when it makes itself heard. It makes me think of all the leaves that
are being stirred, all the dust that is being carried from its resting
place to new adventures, all the water that is being rippled in rivers
and lakes and ocean. And best of all I like to think of its blowing
hard on little birds' wings. I think they like the struggle.

A WOODS VOICE

A far-, far-away sound, a long way off in the woods beyond the
upper end of my pond, tonight. One would have said that a youngster was crying, over and over again. But there is no house within
hearing in that direction. I listened again and realized that it was
a little owl out hunting. The sound was not that of crying at all
but just the owl's way of singing as he went about the task of
finding supper, or whatever the owl's evening meal should be called.
Breakfast, I suppose!

CHRYSANTHEMUM

I wonder how many petals a large chrysanthemum unfolds at its
full growth! At the moment I am too lazy to count them. Later I
shall. I have been looking at a large full bloom beside me in a vase.
Isn't it compact! It seems to me to be a trifle—well—bold. I almost expect to see an impertinent tongue appear from between its
full cheeks.

ABSORPTION

What a potent attraction there is in watching somebody do
something! It is completely immaterial what it is that's being done.
Painting a picture, erecting a girder, or just digging a hole—the
fascination is sure. It is quite unnecessary that the undertaking
have any connection with the needs or activities of the beholder.
Today I saw at least twenty-five men (and two women) crowded
around a man demonstrating a liquid that would "nickel-plate"
the reflector of a motor-car headlight. All were intently absorbed
in the very simple and seemingly prosy process as the man smeared

the stuff on an then polished a little section of the metal with a dirty rag. Probably not one in the whole fascinated crowd had more than a remote use for such a substance.

Interesting, inexplicable human beings!

FALLEN LEAVES

I hope that you will notice the under part of the leaves, fallen leaves, as I have been seeing them these past few days. In all nature there is no equal for those soft shades, all tinged with silver, that are unnoticed almost always, I am sure. I stood by some last evening to drink in the loveliness of their color and their fragrance. It was a real Autumn moment.

IT WILL BE DAWN

Later I shall find you,
In a century yet to come.
Together we shall seek the dew
Of a new life's dawn.
We'll touch the drops with finger tips,
And where they lie in hollow rocks
We'll sip, with laughter on our lips.
It will be dawn!
We'll go to meet the day—but first,
By the rising sun,
We'll pause, my Love, to quench our thirst.

BACH

Last night Bach's "Great Fugue" in G minor. When I hear Bach's music I want to pray, to worship. There is a dignity, a sublimity, a soaring tribute about some of his writings to which I respond with every fibre of my soul. The Fugue last night, arranged admirably for orchestra, retranslated to the organ in my own mind, left me figuratively on my knees.

PIGEONS

I want to tell you about pigeons.

You know how quickly they can rise from the ground and gain altitude. I have been reading about that, and about a pigeon's arrangement of wing muscles. They have especially powerful muscles for lifting their bodies—so strong and large that sometimes a half of the entire weight of a pigeon is accounted for by just the two sets of muscles that are attached to the wings—the set for lowering the wings and the set for raising them.

Soaring birds have an entirely different distribution of power and weight. They, of course, sustain themselves by utilization of air currents, by balancing their bodies on the invisible flow of the swiftly passing air. Their manner of flight is keyed to the extent of their wing expanse. A pigeon, too, can soar at times. But that is only for brief periods and when in rapid motion.

And did you know that birds with rapid lifting power, such as pigeons, have a complex movement in the upstroke of the wing? The inner half of the wing, the part nearest the body, rises first, while the outer half is still depressed. Then the outer half follows. In that way there is less air-resistance to the rise of the wing.

PIRATES

Why is it that although pirates are very improper persons, notoriously bad, completely lawless, all of us like to read about them and hear about them and see them dramatized whenever possible? Perhaps they are, after all, an expression of some of our inner desires.

DEVIL'S CLUB

Every now and then a vivid recollection comes to me of the Devil's Club that I saw growing in the midst of the forests of the Alaskan coast. The plant haunts my memory—its broad green leaves, its thick, resilient stem—all this armed with the most wicked, raking spines. It seemed when I saw it like a vicious outlaw, an ingrate imposing its unwelcome company upon the great peaceful trees around it and their attendant ferns and mosses.

I have seen many thorny and wicked plants in the desert, some of them worse than the Devil's Club. But there I expected them and did not find them incongruous. There the conditions were all in keeping. All living things had to fight for their existence, and all had developed efficient weapons.

Of course the Devil's Club merely has had to insure its own existence. It would be easy forage for animals of the forest, were it not for the spines. Its leaves, very broad that they may gather enough light in the dimness beneath the great crowns above them, are attractive. Its stem is succulent. It could never have survived without protection, and it has achieved this through thorns, as have so many other plants.

The thrill and romance and beauty of a fire to sit before and to watch! The human race has cherished its home fires for so many thousands of years that it may rightly look upon its love of them as a part of its very blood.

PROCESSION

How smoothly and beautifully and appallingly the days and months flow past! Tonight my feet rustle fallen leaves, trees in my woods carry the remnants of russet banners, the evening sky shows those crisp orange and green tints that come only with late autumn sunsets. Yesterday the horse-chestnut buds were swelling with young and eager leaves, the willow shoots were vivid green with new life, the finches were on their way North. It all moves with such incredible, inexorable, magnificent swiftness. Figures in the procession come and go before I am really aware of their presence.

It leaves its heritage—all the rich store of scenes and events. The significant and lovely experiences are not lost, of course. They will remain. That, I think, is one of the priceless privileges of being a human creature, of having the ability consciously to remember.

VERMONT

Don't you think that it must be a rich and pleasant experience to be a tree in this country of the Vermont mountains? Earth and sky and clouds and streams, all are kind to trees here and bid them welcome. The ice-cap, when it melted away, left the land prepared for them. Away back of that the forces that laid down the rocks must have mixed into their substance the ingredients that trees would like and need.

They are such a richly varied company here! Out West they would not grow that way. There a whole section of mountain-side would be occupied by only one kind, each the same as its neighbors. Here for the most part various evergreens and hardwoods, shrubs and little plants, grow in one another's company. Of course if a white spruce desires only white spruce around it, the matter can be arranged. If a cedar wishes for it, there are good, rank-smelling swamps. But the custom is the other way.

Here, where I am writing, mists and rains have prevailed for three or four days. They must have seemed grateful. When Winter comes the deep snow must be a fine and welcome protection for the myriad little roots that later will have work to do. Everything is right. There are no avalanches to gash the forest. When strong winds blow, each tree has the help of its fellows, big and little, to enable it to hold its footing against the violence.

When a tree grows old and gives up life it has not yet reached the end. Its substance will come in time to nurture other generations that will follow through the years.

It seems to me that through it all there is a richness and a peace. I like to look upon it and think of it and feel it.

ONE HOUR

I saw thee on thy horse
Come rushing o'er the plain.
I heard thee tap on my door.
One hour! Thou were't gone again.

I saw thee ride away.
And lo!, there seemed to be
A woman riding behind,
Along on the horse with thee.

Her forehead touched thy back.
Her arms embraced thy sides.
She rode, a part of thy form,
In tune with the horse's strides.

The violet dusk grew dim.
The hills held purple light.
Thy trail led out to the West
And on, to the wistful night.

I watched thee disappear.
And lo!, it came to me—
The woman there on the horse
Was I—and I rode with thee!

WILDERNESS FREEDOM

I wonder if a very real part of the appeal in returning for a period to a sort of wilderness existence may not lie in the fact that for that period one may genuinely choose the place and time and order of one's activities.

It seems to me that the human beings are rare who control their hours. I am due at my office at a certain time. Mail arrives. Dictations follow. Meetings and conferences come along in their magnificently uncontrollable sequence. I go to lunch. I go to dinner. I go to bed. Most of it with about as much real choice on my part as there would be in trying to choose the course of the moon!

But let me have a day or a week in the woods. I can choose then where I shall be or not be, what I shall do or not do, and when I shall do it and how. In a single hour I have more of the joy of being my own master than I can have in a month elsewhere.

The pleasure of it lies not alone in one's major activities. Equally, I think, it is to be found in little things—in the way I may sit, or recline if I choose, in the comfortable crushed state of my hat, in my relationship with the chipmunk who finds me now a trustworthy part of my surroundings, in that untroubled acceptance of the passage of time which gives no heed to schedules but lets the minutes run their free and good course.

There's something fundamental about it all, and something healing and restoring and right.

WET PAWS

This morning I saw a small, brown, mongrel dog playing with the ocean. He was all alone on the wide and long stretch of beach. Every few moments he made a fierce attack on an incoming wave, with no results except two (and every other wave or so, four) wet paws. He was filled with energy and purpose, but I know that eventually he found out that the sea was something he couldn't shake.

THE RIPPLING BREATH

I think that I should like to kneel
Upon hushed, leaf-strewn ground and feel
A low-voiced wind pass close to me.

I think that I should like to see
Its gently rippling breath bestir
A sleeping rabbit's soft white fur.

A PLEA

I wish that present-day astronomers would think up for me a new symbol for the distances in space that they are talking about.

After a good deal of practice I have acquired a reasonable composure in considering the space-measure that they term a "light-year." I don't really and actually grasp the thing in the way of concretely sensing it, but I can manage a certain dizzy comprehension of its elements.

A "year" for instance is definite enough. That part is all right. Next, of course, you must grasp the fact that light travels 186,000 miles a second. Now 186,000 miles as a distance is fairly comprehensible, though I have trouble in conceiving of light or anything else moving so fast that in the blink of a single second it can reach a point nearly 200,000 miles away. The relation of a single second to a whole year is magnificently difficult, but I know what a second is and I can conceive of an enormous lot of them as stringing along into minutes, hours, days, and eventually a year.

These elements are, in a way, mentally manageable. When I combine them I arrive at a sort of vaguely usable notion, although I feel like one who is attempting to toss planets about on his fingertips.

But when they begin talking of light-years in terms of millions I am lost. For example, I have no satisfactory idea of a hundred million. The statement that a galaxy is 200 million light-years distant from me amounts to no more in my poor mind than so many numerals. They've brought in a factor that I can't comprehend and are using it to multiply something that was breathless enough already.

I wish that the astronomers would give me something that I can use.

GLACIER

Mendenhall Glacier is before me—a shining front and swelling surface of white ice, all thrown up in folds and pinnacles. Its face extends to a far-off rocky rampart, and its body, coming from some hidden source higher up in the range, flows around a nearby mountain on its way to the spot where I stand.

It seems almost visibly to flow, like some enormous mass of semi-fluid substance, as if a giant of the mountains had made up a prodigious, crystalline, liquid matrix and had poured it out in the midst of the peaks—poured it in such liberal quantity that the mountain canyons could not contain it, so that it ran over and spread out on the face of the world.

SONG

Clear, sparkling, cold little brook that starts from this foot-hill, here behind my cabin, this mountain slope, to make its journey all the way down to the ocean!

When it is farther along in its travels it will have to withstand all sorts of difficulties and indignities that men will subject it to—dirt from plowed fields, and even poisonous chemicals that will make it unable to serve as the home for fishes and water plants. But here it is as it was meant to be.

And the song it sings is its own traditional music, sung by brooks since the first land appeared in all the world—a song more ancient than any other on earth, unless it be that of the wind and of breaking waves.

INVISIBLE LIFE

I am sitting where I can look out on sloping bank, hillside, woods, and distant mountains. A drift of white snow is near at hand. Above it lies the fallen trunk of a pine tree, supported by the stubs of old, broken branches. In the tangle of woodland growth all around stand spruces with scaly bark and white patches of gum, birches in little squadrons like white-clad special citizenry, young beech trees holding tight to their garments of brown leaves, little pines that look as if they had been growing too fast for their clothes and needed to acquire more extensive garments for their slender necks and shoulders, a wild cherry with a ruddy trunk like dregs of wine.

The air is cold and still. Only the brown beech leaves with their broad curled surfaces and their slender flexible stems betray the occasional touch of lightest breeze.

Everything seems immobile, as if in the winter's cold all life had been locked up, rendered impotent, abstracted until a warmer time of year would permit its restoration. It is as if all processes of growth and activity had been suspended, as if the visible, hard, frozen ground represented the invisible inner state of all things, great and small, within sweep of my eyes, as if winter meant cessation, void, negation.

And yet, in no least spot in all that I can see has vital activity actually been suspended. Its ordinary outward manifestations are altered or absent. But its processes and wonders go on, as intricately and exquisitely as the more rapid and more familiar activities of summer.

A few yards below me ice covers a woodland pool. I walked down to look at it and found that it was by no means the frigid encasement of a lifeless basin, but rather the transparent covering that the cold had built over a crystal bowl of living water. Around the bowl the frozen ground gave no hint of the secret channels by which the water was finding its way to this outlet. But leaves rested lightly in the bottom of the pool, as they do in any flowing spring. The cover of ice was very thin because the living water in it was constantly renewed from channels too far beneath the surface of the ground to know that this is December. Out from the lower margin of the pool flowed a brisk, vocal stream, a stream that would defy Winter every foot of the way, every moment of time, until it reached the ocean.

I could not gather the leaves lightly poised in the bottom of the pool to look at them, nor could I reach the ooze beneath them, but I know that if I could I should find a host of tiny living creatures. I know that in the stream flowing from the basin other creatures are living, that farther along trout are swimming and going about their daily affairs, breasting the current, pursuing one another, finding things to eat.

The old fallen pine tree above the snow bank appears lifeless, a dead shell of what was once the strong framework of a vigorous tree. But I know that within the old trunk equally intricate life goes on, even now. Borers are there, converting the wood cells into new material for new little trees. A myriad of microscopic organisms are at work, or if today in the low temperature their activities are altered for the moment, nevertheless within their small bodies something equally potent and exquisite continues, if I could but see and understand.

The spruce needles and the pine needles, glossy, solid, functioning in their own secret way,—they have not abandoned their life and activity because Winter is here and the air is cold and the ground is frozen. Nor have the twigs and branches and trunks. Nor the bushes with their sprawling frame-work. Nor the water beneath the ice. All around me life goes on—silent to my ears because they are not attuned to catch it, invisible to my eyes because they do not know how to see it, undisclosed to my mind because I do not know how to read the story.

MIST AT DAWN

Misty earth at dawn,
Cloaked in tenuous drift,
Sending skyward your gift,
Lazily,
Hazily,
Pause and let my soul drink!
Pause and let my mind think!
Pause that my eyes may see
Loveliness set free!

FEATHER

I have found something to match the unbelievable multitude of florets in a blossom of Queen Anne's Lace or a golden-rod bloom. Listen to this.

A bird's primary feather—one of the feathers most used in flight—has of course a central shaft. From this shaft other small shafts, called "barbs," branch off—a large number of them. But that is not all. From each barb still smaller little branches arise, called "barbules." A single feather of a pigeon, just one of its primaries, may have nearly a million of these barbules!

PROUD BEGGARS

Beggars are they who come to me,
Beggars, Ah Yes!, but utterly free
Of whimpering, cringing beggary.

Eagerly down to my feeding tray,
Eagerly comes this glad array
Of Junco, and Sparrow, and gaudy Jay.

Proud as the kings of Aztec days,
Proud with a pride lost in a maze
Of myriad, dainty, graceful ways.

Grateful are they for what I do,
Grateful, perhaps! I wish I knew.
But then my longings for thanks are few.

Payment they give, this winged throng,
Payment they give the whole day long
In whispering wings and liquid song.

Servant am I at their command.
Servant, Ah Yes! At each demand
I come with giving, outstretched hand.

Glad shall I be if they stay with me.
Glad shall I be if I'm never free
Of radiant, glowing beggary.

CAROL

A little while ago, when I walked into the big concourse of Grand Central, I heard voices singing. There was a quartet or double quartet in the high-up balcony at one end. They were very good voices, and they were singing the carol "Jerusalem."

What a different note it was in this great station! There was something almost creepily beautiful about it.

MOUNTAIN TOP

I wish that I might stand on a high mountain, a firm one of black basalt, something strong and elemental, not a crumbling shale slope. I want to stand on its very top and I want a chill wind to blow strongly about me. I want white clouds to rush by in the sky. I want to look down and see silent bits of water, silent woodlands. I want to see no human beings, nor do I want to be conscious of the possibility of their approach. I want to see no cattle, no houses, no smoke from chimneys. After I have been on this high, beautiful mountain and feasted my eyes on nothingness for a long, long time, I should like some wild creature to draw near and in some way let me know that I have brought nothing of the confusion of my world into his. Then I want the day to become night. I want the stars and moon to come—then the dawn.

WOOD

I think that things made of metal can never have just the same kind of appeal as things made of wood or other material that is as it

grew. Metal means something made by man—something smelted and poured and rolled and hammered—not something with growth rings and natural texture and pattern.

TWO MEN IN AN ELEVATOR

We have been visiting a department store, going from pillar to post in search of something. Each time, after a long wait, a large elevator would appear. Persons inside would gradually make up their minds whether to get out or not. Presently we would get in, and the operator would invite us to step to the rear, please, and unwillingly we would do so. At our floor we would hopefully wait while women in front of us tried to decide whether they wished to get out or not and meanwhile effectively blocked our intended exit. We'd work our way through other women who were desirous of getting in. Finally having arrived at last at the completely hidden department that we were seeking, and having discovered that what we wanted was not to be had there, we departed from the place by way of a stairway.

STOVE

A plain, unadorned thing, this stove of mine here in my cabin. But it fills its place in existence, dependably and well. If you peep through the chink in the top of it you can see a lively life in progress within—flames dancing and sparks whirling—and if you listen silently for a moment you can hear it talking to itself.

SPACE

Distant stars tonight. Jupiter is nearer than all the rest—slightly too proud, I think, in his manner—but then he is Jupiter!

Is there not some way by which a human being can get a little nearer to the rest of the Universe? Are all human beings forever and ever doomed to know as little about the stars and planets as we do now—to be always so far away from them, to be so mystified by their orderly deportment? I want to know badly.

THE UNKNOWABLE

I have been thinking about the influences—the unknowable influences—exerted by a human life.

I suppose that every man who has reached the latter years of his life, if he is a thinking man at all, must sometimes say to himself "What have I done that can be of any possible significance or permanence in this vast world? Even in my own small part of the world, what have I built that will last?" I suspect that the greater the man's work in the eyes of those about him, the greater also the question in his secret mind, for he will be one who thinks more deeply and more searchingly. The business that he has erected, if he is a business man, he knows will cease to exist in time. His professional work, if he is a professional man, will be forgotten. No matter what the nature of his activities, that which he looks upon cannot be other than fleeting. Or so it seems.

But is that all? Is it even the greater part? I do not believe that it is.

I have been thinking of a tree—a tree that has lived its slow, steady life in its own place until now it has passed the zenith of its maturity. If it could think and if it could talk, it might well say "Here I have stood through a hundred years. I have followed my cycle of seasonal rest and activity. I have grown to the accepted size of trees of my kind. Presently, now, I shall reach the end of my life. And that is the whole story."

But the tree could not know that its strong roots, binding the soil, turned aside a stream that later, in its further course, would have destroyed a countryside. It could not know that beneath its shelter rested a traveller who, one day, because of that rest, led his countrymen to new vision and freedom. It could not know any one of a thousand events that took place because of its existence.

So, too, not one of us can ever possibly know all that flows from our personal existence. What we do know, if we stop to think about it, is that no force, once set moving, comes to an end; that all we do, every bit of it, is inevitably the beginning of widening circles. To judge only by that which we can see is to forget that which we cannot see. And the latter must of necessity be the greater part.

I think that what we can see does not really much matter. It is temporal and passing. It cannot be otherwise. If that were all of it the question that a man asks of himself would answer itself—and the answer would be a negation of the wish and longing that prompted the question. The *real* answer, hidden and unknowable though it be, may well be a glory of fulfillment.

Many men whose names have come down through the centuries thought their life futile. *We* know that what they did was the very opposite of futility. Many more have remained unknown. But what they did was a widening circle, unknown to them in all its ultimate consequences, but real.

BONDAGE

Let me take into my eager hands
Thy soul, and spin from it in triple strands
The priceless threads of body, spirit, mind.
Let me weave these threads until they blend
Into a cord that flows without an end.
Let me pause a little while to rest,
And as I lean against thine own dear breast,
Bewildered by the wonders that I find,
Take the bond that is a part of thee
And make, my Love, a prisoner of me!

DIATOMS

Never have I seen anything so geometrically perfect, so awe-inspiring in their minute forms, as those hundreds of diatoms crowded in that one small spot beneath my microscope lens!

It seems unfathomable that any Order in Nature, any Unknown in the universe, any Guiding Mentality, could have conceived and produced such almost invisible beauty.

FADS AND FUNDAMENTALS

I suppose that fads are to be expected at times in the arts. We had the cubist in pictorial art, though seemingly the cult did not prevail long. We have had grotesque, blatant, repellant styles in murals. We have had a fad in music, and we still have some of it. We have had a fad, and still have it, in poetry.

It seems to me that in all the creative arts there are fundamentals that cannot change—beauty that is based on simplicity and purity of form and structure—work that is the expression of some universal emotion or experience or aspiration—truth that is imbued with life—imagination that speaks an understandable language. Sometimes those who wish to create seem to forget these, or to violate them for the sake of notoriety, or to deny them in an endeavor to be "original." But all the time the really great creative artists, painters and composers and writers, go quietly on. And all the time, I think, they remain the enduring influence, because what they are doing is based on fundamental rightness.

MUSING

How would you like to be sitting beside some faroff stream this afternoon, watching bubbles float past, and water striders journeying here and there?

MACAW

I would give much to know what impressions, what dim or bright records of experiences, hovered in the head of a white macaw that I visited, in the big zoological gardens at Washington.

For more than forty years he has been a resident of that zoo, and today, they tell me, he is the surviving pioneer, at the top of the list in point of service. No other creature in all the vast place has been there as long as he. A little sign on the front of his cage attests his service.

He is just within the entrance of a room in a big building where the birds live who must have warmth through the winter months. You might pass him by without noting him, on your way to a huge and alluring flying cage where even sea-gulls wing about. But if he chooses he can make you aware of his presence. He has a potent voice.

I suppose that hundreds of thousands of visitors have lingered before his domain, watching his sure, deliberate, original methods of climbing up the wire front of his cage, and in turn being scrutinized by his bright, inquisitive, appraising eyes. Some of them know him well. I think that his list of acquaintances must be very large, and I am certain that it must be exceedingly varied.

When I stood in front of his cage he looked me over intently. It was impossible not to feel that he was examining me as a human specimen and arriving at his own conclusions about me. He was clinging to the wires, peering out between them, and his whole demeanor was one of capable and experienced scrutiny. I moved close to the cage and began to talk to him, and he gave all the more impression of sizing me up, deliberately and thoroughly. When I moved to one side, out of view, he shifted his position so as to peer around the corner. When I came back he acted as if, with a little further acquaintanceship, he would be ready to sit down and discuss with me all sorts of topics of mutual interest.

I wish that I knew what was in his head. Vague, formless impressions perhaps—but he didn't look it. He looked like one who, in his own way, knew more than a good many human beings—the subway readers of tabloids for example. I wish that I knew.

SMOKE

Smoke, so stealthy in your flight
Across the star-strewn void of night,
Pale against the indigo
That spreads blue darkness over space,
Soft your footsteps, brief your trace!

Low your fragile spirals flow
In vap'rous upward trail, until
Death draws nigh, and all is still.

I wonder whither you were bound,
What you sought and would have found
If winds had granted longer life.
I wonder if you would have kissed
A cloud—and kept a lover's tryst!

SNOWFLAKES

Tonight I walked home, all the way up the street, with my tongue well out. No one was about, and I wanted to see how those soft, white snowflakes felt upon my tongue, and how they tasted. There were so many of them in the air that I could not be sure whether they were falling up or down.

Here is an addition for the list of original ladies:

Along with several other pedestrians I was standing in the middle of a New York street, waiting for the lights to change and the traffic to pause. The whole street everywhere was encased in ice, all in hills and valleys, and as slippery as ice could be.

A man who was waiting a short distance away started to go ahead, regardless of the red light, and promptly went down on all fours in a glassy rut. A big truck bore down on him, brakes set and wheels sliding. The man in the rut could not get up. He was short and stout, and his feet were going wildly but getting him nowhere. Finally, in the nick of time, the truck stopped sliding and the man got to his feet and stood rubbing his wet hands.

At this point a rangy, horsey-looking woman in my group walked over to the man, said something, and came back. I must have looked my inquiry, for she leaned over toward me and said, in an air of complete conviction, "I told him that his time hadn't come yet."

FAR STARS

Far Stars, sing a lullaby
In rhythm with the deep night sky!
Send thy music to my ears!
Send it on the long light years!
Let the moons of Saturn be
Part of thy soft song to me.
Weave into thy lullaby
Mists from all the nebulae.
Sing, Far Stars, and I shall be
A listener to thy melody!

FINDING A CAMP SITE

I think that among all the experiences and adventures that come to one in a wilderness journey there is none that is more alluring, more provocative and yet satisfying, more fully remembered afterwards in all its.details, than is the undertaking of finding the right spot for an overnight camp and then fitting oneself and one's needs and wishes into its offering.

In a canoe trip the adventure is at its best. The course of travel automatically presents successive scenes and possibilities. In fact it begins to do this from the moment you set out upon a given day's journey. The first bend that you pass in your stream, or the first point that you round, discloses a spot with multiple attractions openly displayed. The earlier in the day this takes place the more extensive and manifest the advantages. The bank is well above the water but not too high, the approach to it is easy, the trees upon it are noble and rightly arranged, the view from it is undoubtedly superb, the shore at its foot offers a bit of gently sloping, sandy beach, and just beyond there is a cove where there must be a spring or an entering brook. Neighboring hardwoods promise excellent dry fuel. Beyond question it is the best spot that you have ever seen, and you leave it with the feeling that you have forever missed something out of life.

In the course of the next hour half-a-dozen others pass in review. The country is full of them. You have a conviction that this lavishness is not going to last. It is going to be followed later by a dearth. But the day is young, your final objective lies many miles ahead, and you can't stop to spend the night at every promising bank or knoll.

A dearth does follow, all through the middle of the day. The shores become low and swampy-looking, or excessively rocky, with no offering of a decently dry or level place for a tent. This seems to run on indefinitely. The sun is half-way to the western horizon. The map indicates nothing that anybody has found worth recording.

At four o'clock you observe a place that looks half promising, but no more. It is not as high above the water as it should be, and the trees upon it are too thick and too small. It would do, in a way. There may be nothing better ahead before dark. While you are debating it the current carries you by, and half in relief, half in premonition of difficulty, you decide not to paddle back.

Another hour presents nothing that is even half promising. You quicken the stroke of your paddle. You hurry, and watch the declining sun, and grow hopeless and morose.

Then suddenly you come upon the spot, the right spot, the most completely right spot that anyone could ask for. It stands up against the forest background, and the level sun-rays shine into it and make splashes on its big tree-trunks. There is a beach. There is a cove. There is firewood. There are saplings for tent-poles and stakes. You put ashore and haul up, and as you walk about on the smooth ground under the trees, mentally placing tents and fire, you know that you have arrived at one more camp-site that you will have always with you, along with all the others of other streams and lakes and years.

LIFETIME

Mountains are in sight now—blue and white—a long, knobby, jagged line of them. What hidden secrets of valleys and streams, forests and snow, they hold! A thousand places lie there to be explored. All one needs is just a life-time to do it in, and some food and clothing and shelter—and that companionship in quest and in enjoyment of it all that would transform the impossible into the possible.

MID-WESTERNERS

Whenever I visit the mid-West I find a certain characteristic that is good to think about and to carry away in thought—and that is the attitude of people toward their neighbors and friends and chance acquaintances.

They *are* friendly—sympathetically, understandingly, generously friendly. It is a marked characteristic. It has often been spoken of as a friendliness toward strangers, but it is deeper and wider than that. It is not just a surface matter, and it is not merely an effort to make the stranger welcome. It is a patient, generous understanding toward one another, toward any human being. It is everywhere in evidence, and it is completely at the opposite pole from the hard, unresponsive attitude that seems to appear sometimes in other sections, and perhaps in other and older countries. There is no class distinction in the mid-West. And, still deeper, there seems to be no feeling of superiority, no impatience, no wall around oneself.

I went into a railway station to make a reservation. An elderly woman was ahead of me. She was discussing with the agent her coming journey to the West Coast. The matter involved a possible change of route so that she might be able to stop off and see friends at some point. The agent worked it out carefully and sympathetically with her, as if it were his own trip that was under consideration. Another woman, next in line, was patient. No one could be otherwise in that atmosphere.

In another station I myself had inquiries to make. The agent was equally kind and friendly with me. It was not that he had nothing else to do, or that travellers were so scarce as to be welcome merely as some one to talk with. It was an inner attitude, a customary way.

I saw the same thing everywhere, in every sort of human contact. I think that in some fashion or other it has come to be the underlying basis of human relationship. And I think that it is a fine and admirable quality.

BUOYANCY

What power lies in one's inner spirit!

If I could have just one wish granted, just one, as regards my own personal estate and makeup and qualities, I think that I should ask that every minute, so long as life lasts, buoyancy and confidence and eagerness of spirit remain with me. Then no possible adversity could make any difference—no failure of health, no possible passing of the years, no outward material disaster, no collapse of ambition or plans.

TO A FRIEND

Throughout the firm rock wall
That ever offers all
I crave in staunch support,
Where, grain by grain,
The particles of friendship blend,
There runs a vein,
A band within the quiet quartz,
Of rich, pure ore
That pledges with its hidden depths
A yield of Friendship Wealth
That time can not destroy,
That nothing can alloy!

TO THE MOON

The moon last night! For miles I watched it. There were golden shafts of light, now from the upper curve, now from the lower. And I, a small humble thing of the earth, felt as though I should build a temple somewhere and worship Tanit.

IDIOM

In Philip Hale's book of Symphony Program Notes I found this:

"To begin with, we do not hear music now with the ears of the earlier centuries, and the old idiom to-day has no pertinence except when it has been handed down to us by a master of it who broke through the idiom and made a universal language of it for many years to come."

It left me pondering. At first I could not accept "we do not hear with the ears of the earlier centuries." People change so little, fundamentally, during thousands upon thousands of years! But now I think that I understand. I know in my heart that it is the rare bit of creative work that is universal and touched with perpetuity.

WINTER BEACH

What treasures are spread on a winter beach! Bright, smooth stones—broken shells, black, white, and iridescent, and once in a while one of beautifully curled form—trail-marks where the tide

has drawn seaweed over the sands—pools here and there where some wave could not entirely escape. Above it all a clear sky with cloud tracings in the East. And everywhere the salt fragrance that belongs to the sea alone.

FIDGETS

Why is it that when one *must* sit still and quiet in a room, facing other people, and listen to out-loud reading, one wants to fidget? That happened to me last night.

First I squirmed about until my dress crept to my knees. Then I pulled that down. Then I decided my back was tired, so I slipped down on the middle of my spine, only to find that I had been more comfortable sitting upright. (But I couldn't move, for I just had.) Then I wanted to cough but decided to wait, which I did. Then I thought that it would be the height of delight to sit on my foot. I finally did, only to discover that it should have been the other foot. Then I *thought* yawns until I became uncontrollable. Then my mind wandered from the spoken word to remote ideas until I was made aware of my dreaming by some polite burst of laughter. Then I rubbed my hands over my face and through my hair until I became conscious of having done it, and felt in consequence like some untidy hyena.

LEADERSHIP

I have been reflecting on the influence that a man who is in a position of leadership can exert upon a people through his own adherence to ideals. It seems to me that the silent power of such a man is far-reaching, and that of all persons a man who is at the head of government, the ruler, can exert the widest and deepest influence. By the simple example of his own life he can define for many people the worthy and enduring ideals—and such definition often is needed.

Temporal, physical welfare defines itself. It needs no emphasis. Every man knows when he is well fed, knows when he enjoys luxuries, knows what they are and what they mean. The kind of house he lives in, the amount of money that he earns—these need no interpreter. The advantage of a greater income and its ability to secure for him greater physical comforts—all this is plain.

Not only are these advantages self-evident, but constantly every man is under pressure to give them greater space in his thoughts and aims. Every page of every newspaper, of every magazine, tells the people over and over what they may have in the way of more luxuries. Much of the emphasis in education, as we have it today, is in the same direction. Sometimes much of the emphasis in governmental planning may lead toward the same end.

Yet those who have thought human life through, broadly and wisely, know that the most rewarding aims do not lie in the realm of physical luxuries at all. They lie in a different field, and they look to ideals that are far less obvious, far harder to define, far more difficult to make clear. They may seem to involve self-denial, self-discipline, the giving up of the immediate and tangible for that which is indefinite, almost unworldly. And yet they are real and enduring.

For many, I think, a potent influence in defining ideals, perhaps the most potent or the only influence, lies in the example of the man who, because of his position, occupies a place of respect and authority. In smaller groups the head of an enterprise for which men work, the president of a company for example, possesses the power to create standards for those who work for him. He need not speak of them. He need not urge them. And perhaps if he is wise he will never do so. But the power and influence are there, just the same. In a tremendously larger way the man who stands at the head of a whole country can define ideals for millions. He again may never speak of them. But to great numbers of people his example in itself creates standards and crystallizes ideals in almost every aspect of human living.

I think that one of the great privileges of being a king or an emperor, if a wise and worthy king or emperor, must have been the knowledge that among countless subjects the creation of sound ideals lay within the power of one man's life and example.

WAS IT A FLOCK OF GULLS

Was it a flock of gulls that rose
In a flight so swift and so free
From the salt marsh, there by the sea,
From the frozen crest of the winding stream
Where the yellow grasses in glacial dream
Wait with their slanting tips pressed fast,
Captives in ice while north winds last?
Was it a flock of gulls that rose?
Who knows—who knows!
Or was it a sigh from the spirit of light,
That tenuous flight of white from white?

UNFOLDING

This March morning—a chipmunk! He came out and sat upon a stone and quietly surveyed the snowy landscape. After a while he disappeared under the woodshed, then came out in a new place, again went "below," and once more emerged and sat upon his stone.

I wonder what it felt like to him to sit beneath the open sky after his months in some dark, warm, hidden shelter, and what it felt like to renew acquaintance with pleasant, convenient holes into which to dodge, and with runways along which to scamper. I wonder what sort of internal alarm-clock it was that set him off, whereas at an earlier date, although the temperature was higher on occasion, he did not come out, so far as I know.

This morning also some robins in an apple tree. They did not sing to the morning light as they will later. Not time yet for the vocal accompaniment to wooing and mating and nesting. But they were robins and their breasts were ruddy, though dull, and they said silently "The life of spring with all its outpourings is soon to be here."

I welcome profoundly this invitation to share again in the unfolding of the myriad-sided outdoors.

MY BOWL OF PHOENICIAN GLASS

If I could whisper to the dead,
To him who made my bowl of glass,
One who perhaps saw Jesus pass
With burdened head,
I'd tell
How even now his work exists,
How all its loveliness persists,
How time has but enhanced its spell.
I'd let him know
That iridescent colors dress
The sloping sides he chose to press,
That now it bears a centuries' glow.
And I'd say
That long it hid beneath the ground,
Where fate ordained that it be found
Within my span of life, my day.
I'd whisper to the dead
That all the melody of line
Of his creation now is mine;
That all the beauty of his bowl
Now calms a hunger in my soul.

TULIPS

Last night moonlight came through the window and fell upon some potted tulips. The blossoms were full blown. It seemed to me that they had flung back their arms with abandon to receive the light. I enjoyed their beauty, their form, and their silvered orange tints.

COMPANY

There was work to do, repairing a feeding-tray. While I worked chickadees paid occasional visits. They were going to another tray that's out in front of the cabin, but they brought sunflower seeds to bushes near me to hammer them open. Often they perched only a few feet away, and always they made remarks. I suspect that they harbor a constant suspicion that their seeds are coveted by the nearby human being. Or is it that they just like company?

CREATIVE WORK

A psalm of five thousand years ago—a melody in F—an Angelus—a poem that gives wings to human spirits—what gift to human beings can be so great as these, and what achievement can equal the creation of such as these?

TESTIMONY

A trial is over, to which I had been summoned to give expert testimony. The whole thing seemed like a contest in which the aim was to win any point that could possibly be won, to cover up any truth that might advantageously be concealed—not like a fair endeavor to find out the facts in a decent and honest way.

Perhaps it is only by this sort of contest that an approximation of justice can be had—but it seems to me to be wrong.

FLORIDA LAGOONS

I have been driving through a vast, level region where there were many grassy openings, with shallow, broad, irregular pools of water in them. In and around these pools were thousands of tall, long-legged water-birds—herons and cranes and their relatives—and occasional ducks. Sometimes I saw a flock all in white, walking around fishing, or covering all the available branches of a bare tree, or flying in a snowy cloud. Sometimes they were all blue, or slate-color. Sometimes the pattern was a mixed one.

There must have been gorgeous fishing in those lagoons and channels—millions of small fishes, and maybe ranks and platoons of frogs or other suitable water creatures. I do not know how many small fish would be considered a satisfactory breakfast in the opinion of a crane or heron, but I'd think that no paltry three or four would do.

If all those birds find it profitable to be here, as presumably they must since they could so easily go elsewhere, the hidden life beneath the water must be even more extensive than the visible life above.

MOON CRATERS

I have been reading about the moon. Did you know that there are craters on the moon that are more than 140 miles across and are 17,000 feet deep? And did you know that when the sun is shining on it the surface of the moon reaches a temperature of 250 degrees F., and when that same surface is in darkness the temperature falls to 150 below zero? All due, of course, to the lack of any atmosphere or any moisture.

EASTER RABBITS

What would the rabbit who loafs near my cabin think if he could look into store windows here in New York just now?

Green rabbits, red rabbits, blue and even purple rabbits! Rabbits dressed in baggy Dutch trousers, in cowboy costume with chaps and revolver and sombrero, in gingham dresses with bonnets and with ribbons tied beneath chins, in red pants and plaid waistcoats! And all around, quantities of hen's eggs.

I do not think that my rabbit's remarks would be appreciative.

THE HERRING RUN

The River is forcing you back
With churning force,
But on and up in your course
You strongly fight
To meet the blade of its might.

Your silvered, slim body is worn,
You cannot hide
The bleeding bruise in your side,
Nor once conceal
The hidden force of your zeal.

The quiet, still pool is ahead,
Your goal, your quest,
A place to mate and to rest.
So—On and try!
Although in trying you die!

LICHENS

I have been learning about lichens. Did you know that all lichens are partnerships—each different kind a different partnership, but all of them a sort of working arrangement between some species of alga and some specific fungus. The alga is held within the fungus threads or its structure—closely associated with it in some definite fashion. The fungus holds and collects the necessary moisture. It gives form and strength, and does the work of attaching the partnership to tree or rock or whatever object the lichen clings to or rests on. The alga provides the essential chlorophyll, manufactured with the aid of light.

Many of the algae live also free—by themselves—but in that event they must have moist situations, and they are easily dislodged. Alone they may live for only a short time. In the partnership their life goes on almost indefinitely.

Some of the lichens send out little colonies—little beginnings of the partnership. The substance of the lichen breaks open here and there, and tiny sections become detached, each section including both fungus and alga. These drift to new places and then settle down and take hold and grow.

Nearly always it is the fungus that gives characteristic shape to the lichen. It is the dominating member of the partnership. But there are species in which the alga takes the lead and determines the structure and form.

Seemingly lichens can withstand prolonged drought. Even in very dry air they can survive for years. If the air has any moisture in it at all the fungus partner is able to take this up and thus keep the alga alive and the partnership active and successful.

SOON

It is almost time for violets and little white flowers on a wood road—

CROWDED HOURS

When we permit ourselves to be excessively and continuously "busy," drinking down the excitement of multiple undertakings, I wonder if we are gaining as much as we lose. I wonder if human beings are really made to live that way. Those who seem to have lived the most natural lives, whether individuals or peoples, have not forever crowded their hours. Unconsciously or deliberately they have left time for other things than tense activity. It is not that they have been mentally and spiritually idle. Their minds and senses have not necessarily been stagnant and unresponsive. They simply have found opportunity to see and hear and think and enjoy.

I believe that, if we would, we could double the richness of the passing day. Perhaps we could multiply it tenfold. I believe that this would be an objective more worth seeking than much that we try so hard to attain.

KNEE-DEEP

The trees are standing to their knees in all the rivers. There seems to be so much more water in the rivers than the trees can drink at the moment. A great waste!

Last night I thought of all the fairy tales I had read.

For a long time a delightful procession passed by in my mind— good fairies and bad gnomes, beautiful princesses and lovely ladies, princes who did fine deeds, animals that were magic in their power, great giants and tiny elves, silver woods, jeweled palaces, wells and roads and woods bewitched until they did astonishing things, strange people and places—all magic, all witchery, all enchantment. No one can ever take these from me. They are in my mind to stay.

"BELOVED ONE"

The words you murmured, meant for me alone,
Still flame and sparkle with bright, fiery tints
And carry in their depths a thousand glints
Of rare strong faith and vivid hope,
Proclaiming love and proving love's far scope.
"Beloved One"—these words in glory rest
Impressed upon my pulsing heart, as though
Great Vulcan, leaving his dark lair,
Had come himself and burned them there
With god-like forging and undying skill,
So that, anon, when this my heart is still,
Your words will linger on in flame, and lie
An ember of our love that will not die.

BLUEBIRD

This morning I was awakened at the rising of the sun by a blue-bird calling from a tree-top near my cabin. A brief, liquid, rich phrase repeated a half-dozen times with silent pauses between. Think what an exquisite greeting to the new day from that feathered creature high up there where he could see the first light of the sun!

There was no repetition of the song later. I suppose that his springs of expression are only just beginning to fill. A month from now they will be overflowing all day long.

PHOTOGRAPHS

Making photographic prints this afternoon from a long series of negatives dating from last summer. Here are some of the subjects:

Deep shadows and bright sunshine in a high-up forest of yellow pine and mountain spruce, where the trees are broadly spaced one from another—
Mountain peaks, partly snowclad, across a mountain meadow rimmed about with evergreens—
A striped squirrel that came to my woodpile—

A beaver dam and a beaver house—
Sheep in a highup mountain park—
Horses (saddled and unsaddled) in the edge of woods—
A hobbled horse hopping 3-legged-like across an opening—
A man drawing up a broad cinch on a very meek-looking white
  horse—
A high-altitude flower that was as big across as my hand, yet on
  a stem no longer than my little finger—
More 12,000 foot mountains, across more nearby park-like open-
  ings, bordered by more forests—

Do you discern any particular reason for my lingering over these
prints as they went through their chemical baths?

BACKGROUNDS

What a compelling force the appeal of the primitive, the simple,
the unmechanized, may be in a man!

Today I have ridden within sight of Henry Ford's vast manufacturing plant—buildings that, I suppose, cover square miles—
employees that are said to total seventy thousand—the last word
in machinery, new, specialized, enormous in extent—the very last
word in industrialism.

And then I visited the "Village," that Henry Ford is getting
together, in the two-hundred-acre space that he has provided for
it. I went through an entrance and climbed into an old-fashioned
closed carriage, a "hack" as it used to be called. We drove off
behind horses. We passed other similar carriages. We began to
visit old buildings, moved from here and there to their new home
in the Village—moved so carefully that nothing about them could
be disturbed.

I wandered about for as long a time as was available, but I
could visit only a small part—an old inn, with its sitting-room and
its parlor which used to be opened only on Sundays—a court-
house where Lincoln practised law—a country store where even the
merchandise was that which that same store offered for sale
seventy-five years ago—a photo studio, still making tintypes—an
apothecary's shop with its post-office in a corner.

I saw Henry Ford, talked with him a moment. Underneath I
seemed to sense the fundamental Ford, a man who at the beginning
worked with his own hands, who is at heart not only an individu-
alist but the individual worker, who today finds satisfaction in
simple things made by men with their own hands after patterns
existing in their own brains, who wants and needs quiet and trees
and a gentle, unhurried life.

All in due time our American cities will come to have the absorbing, intangible age-quality possessed by the cities beyond the oceans. Human use gives a quality that cannot come in any other way. We have not yet reached that estate.

HOUSE REPAIRS

Workmen are like a sort of hurricane, aren't they? To begin with, you don't know when they are going to arrive or how long they are going to stay. And when they do come there's no telling what they will do. They will accomplish certain things, of course, but in doing so they are certain to scatter everything around, and pay no heed to things that shouldn't be touched, and make a muss everywhere, and leave a sort of trail of destruction behind them. Arranging with masons or builders to do something desired is about like making a contract with a tornado.

IF ONE COULD—

What would it be like to stop being a responsible person? There are times when I'd like to do something of the kind. I don't mean that I want to go out and break all the statutes merely because they are statutes. I mean just not being responsible for anything or anybody.

For instance, I think I'd start by eliminating making a living. Admittedly the money now in my pocket wouldn't buy food for very long. But I wouldn't pay any attention to that. To do so would be to take on again a sense of responsibility. In fact having more money in my pocket might mean trying to stretch it to cover a calculated length of time—and that would be fatal.

If I owed any money, or was going to owe any in the future, or to have any other financial obligation—rent, or insurance, or taxes, or anything else—automatically all that would cease to exist. As one who had stopped being a responsible person I would naturally have nothing more to do with such matters, and therefore they would have no claim on me. Having no claim they would not interest me. And in the same way, I would have no concern as to money that I had invested. If I did I'd be taking on responsibility again—and being responsible to a bond or to a stock certificate would surely be worse than almost any other kind of obligation.

I would cease being obliged to do what I do not want to do, such as all the duties relating to holding down a job, for of course I would not have a job. That in itself would release to me many golden hours of each day. Those hours seem not to be mine at all now. They belong to the job. I am not able to make use of them. The job owns them.

Then, with these hours added to the rest of the twenty-four, I would set out to do what I most wanted to do. Not having any responsibility, I could do that. Perhaps I would starve or grow ill or die. But that would not be of consequence in this revised order of living. Taking that into account would only be going back into responsibilities.

It's curious, isn't it, what notions arise with the first warm days of Spring———

DAWN

The first dim hours of each new day are mine—
The sleeping world has given them to me—
Those hours when all alone I watch the sea
Of rainbow dawn in bands of changing line
Against the eastern sky, as day is born.
A time when tired stars and weary moon
Look down upon the earth with languid smiles
And whisper, "Gone is night. The East grows bright."
A time when some true, grateful well of joy
Bestirs the throats of birds to songs divine
That blend into a silent song of mine!

NORTHLAND

If I were to speak of the books that give me the greatest pleasure I should say "books of Arctic adventure and exploration."

Last night I began the "Saga of Nansen" and travelled with him over the glaciers of Greenland, through nights filled with Aurora lights and swift, cold wind. Did you know that the Eskimo believes that the Aurora Borealis is a game that is played by their dead?

You would like a sentence in that part of the book where Nansen recounts his early outdoor life—"When the oak leaves are like a mouse's ear, then the trout will jump for a fly."

OLD AGE

On the way to Philadelphia today I sat for a while with an elderly gentleman. He was a good seat-companion, interested in many things, definite in his views on various subjects, completely awake to the world and its doings. After a while I found out that tomorrow will be his birthday. He will be eighty-seven.

He was once frozen into unconsciousness, but they thawed him out. He was once "drowned," but they worked over him and brought him back. He was in an accident and sustained various broken bones in the neighborhood of his left shoulder, but they repaired him. He was in another accident and came out of it with a leg broken in two places, but they fixed that, and although he carries a cane he seems not to use it except as he wishes. He is completely blind in one eye, and the only way he can see with the other is by means of a specially ground lens, but he reads and goes about with seemingly no difficulty and with no reservations.

He has a son who is a high-ranking officer in the Navy, and he has three other children, and he would have enjoyed seeing them on his birthday tomorrow, but "they are busy"—so it's all right.

He knew General Grant, he knew McKinley, he knew other Presidents. He walked many miles with his father to see Lincoln's funeral train. He saw and rode behind the first locomotive ever owned by the Pennsylvania Railroad. It made five or six miles in twenty minutes to a half-hour. He was riding with me today in a train that covered ninety miles in ninety-one minutes, and he found this one equally interesting.

There was no indication but that he was looking forward to many other interesting and thrilling experiences and adventures, through many years to come.

I think that it might be a good idea if various young people were made to follow him around for a few days.

SPRING IN STRANGE PLACES

This is May—"The Moon when the Ponies Shed." The sun does not *rise* these days—it suddenly *appears*.

In what strange places Spring reveals itself!

This morning I saw a tiny cherry tree—a beautiful thing with all its blossoms. It was growing in an ugly back yard, surrounded by the family wash.

I saw a tall, old tree, gorgeous in form and color. (I believe that all the leaves had unfolded just as I came by.) It was growing from the pavement before some tumble-down tenements.

Stretching their heads as high as they could, and probably despairing of being heard and seen, stood a row of poplars with new leaves. They grew in the team-yard of a slaughter house.

Then there were two magnolias, only a few inches high, each bearing beautiful blossoms, young as they were. They grew in the front yard of a factory.

THE CLOSING DOOR

Is it true, by liege lord, that I hear
Dim footsteps afar?
Perhaps they are thine—and so—
I'm leaving my portal ajar.

I'm quickening my fire that reclines
In its smoldering sloth,

Whispering now it must burn
For us both.

Nearer the footsteps! Ah! They have passed!
Night!—and a lone, bluelight star!

I'm quenching the last little flame—
I'm lowering the great iron bar!

AMBER

In my hand I hold a piece of amber in which are imprisoned a tiny fly and a small beetle. I wish that I knew this amber's history. In its early days, when it was just gum upon a tree—what kind of a tree? A lone tree, or were there others about? Was the ocean near? How did the gum happen to form? Was it 'way up on the trunk of the tree or near the earth? Was the gum sweet-smelling, and is that why the flies gathered about? Was the beetle pursuing the fly? On what businesses were these little animals bent when their life ended so badly? Did their lives end at once? (I hope so.) How and when and where did these small bugs of mine become trapped?

PHEASANT

The call of a pheasant, close beneath my window, waked me this morning. A strange, harsh call to our ears, but good to the ears of the quiet-garbed mate that no doubt was nearby. A sound that seems not to be of the same order as any other familiar bird note, and yet it signifies something that is good and of the woods.

WYOMING

In this region of the Continental Divide it is the boundlessness of the country, I think, that reaches most deeply into my being. I do not have this same feeling in other places, except perhaps in the desert. In the Valley of the Yosemite, for example, in spite of the great beauty of it all, there was not the same sweeping appeal that I feel here. I wanted to climb out of it—and even on a day in mid-winter when I was there for a second time, and when deep snow covered everything, I struck out alone over a buried trail that led up toward surrounding heights, and I followed it as far as I could in the time available.

Here in the vast spaces of Wyoming an indescribable sense of satisfaction comes to me.

MONEY

If I were a scissors-grinder, or a peddler, or an umbrella man, I'd know exactly what note my little bell should sound. I'd know because of what I saw a few moments ago on the street here. A man walking along dropped a silver half-dollar. It gave out just one or two little rings as it struck the sidewalk. But instantly every man and woman for yards around stopped and turned and looked.

Isn't it funny that human ears can recognize the note so definitely! Some other sound wouldn't even be heard.

WEE ONE!

When midnight steps softly
And knocks on my door,
Then thou wilt come gently,
As always before,
And bid me awaken
To save thy sweet form,
So small and so shaken,
So swept by the storm.
Thy gown all a-jingle
Will droop with the rain,
Thy flesh all a-tingle
Will seek warmth again.
Sweet Mistress of Moonlight,
For thine own dear sake
I'll watch in the darklight;
Thou'lt find me awake!

PILGRIMAGES

In Yutang's book on China I read this morning a section on the reasons why Buddhism is a powerful factor in Chinese life—and I suppose that means in any life where it has influence at all.

One of the reasons had to do with pilgrimages. It was pointed out that pilgrimages satisfy that feeling of wanderlust, that need of change, which makes life unendurable at times. Spring comes. Devout people (who are really emotional people) start off on a pilgrimage to a *distant* place. They meet and talk with fellow pilgrims. They cross new streams, see new lands—and eventually they reach a lamasary (situated on a high mountain where grandeur is overpowering). They remain with the monks a few days, eating good food, talking, spending a little money. Then they return to their poor lives of cramped outlook and hard work, but with more inner strength for bearing their burdens.

In my estimation the monks are welcome to the gold they collect.

KENTUCKY

This Kentucky country is horse country. It is not gasoline country—at least not this part through which I have been travelling. On horseback here, or in a vehicle drawn by a horse, one could go wherever one wished. The roads would be right. No motor cars. No sudden noises. No disquieting hurry.

It seems to me that there is good reason why Kentucky is devoted to the horse. Reason, too, for the great race-track that my train passed a few minutes ago. Of course the track has another cause for existence in the way of betting on the races—but frankly if betting be allowable, is not a horse race the most logical event on which to lay a wager? If I lived in Kentucky and owned a fast Kentucky horse, or if I were acquainted with one, I'm not sure but that I'd back up my loyalty to him by betting on him. It seems like a sort of indigenous affair under these circumstances.

And afoot in this Kentucky country! Such a trip could not be other than interesting. True, the borders of streams and sometimes the fields are grown up to tall weeds. You would acquire many a burdock souvenir, or beggar's tick, or Spanish needle. But the slopes are inviting. There would be rabbits scampering away, and magnificent Kentucky cardinals. There would be tangles of wild grapes, and many a tall, silvery sycamore. And nowhere would there be sight or sound of truck or rushing passenger car.

QUIET EVENING

I have just walked through the quiet, dark night to my pond. There was no sound except that of faint wind in pine-trees and in the leafy dress of elms and birches. The air was soft—a caressing softness—the gentle air that fills all space before rain comes. Only a few stars managed to shine, and these but dimly through rifts in clouds that were not themselves visible but were spread like a curtain over the sky. On the horizon the lights of towns, a few miles away, cast a glow upon the edges of the curtain.

A night for soft voices—for quiet tread—for unhurried steps.

LEADER

I want to be the leading bird in a group flight—to be at the front of the column, taking the responsibility for the tempo of the flight, its startings and stoppings and its ultimate destination.

I should like to belong to a night-travelling species and fly over a quiet earth, leaving my shadow upon the moon and sailing close to the stars. The feeling would be incomparable.

THOUGHTS

An image of My Own,
Clear as a marble figure
To which the moonbeams loan
A cool and unreal splendor!

An image that reflects
With infinite beguiling
The carriage of his form,
The shadow of his smiling!

As long years drift away
And aging outlines dim,
This image bides with me,
My legacy from him!

OUR BACKGROUND

Doesn't it seem a long, long way from world politics and all the rest of civilization's complexities to thoughts of woods and trees—mountain peaks and trails—remote lakes and trout—pack-horses and mountain meadows—wild flowers and squirrels—whistling marmots and deer-tracks—wood for a camp-fire and water from a swift stream—stars overhead and tree-tops against the sky—pack-bags and tramping shoes—balloon silk and rawhide—glaciers and snow-fields—a log to sit on and another to thatch boughs against— —

Yet all these represent such a tremendous part of the history of the human race, in time and in its activities, as compared to corporations and congresses, appropriations and taxes, trains and cement highways, and all the rest that is giving all of us so much concern.

PYRAMIDS

Did you know that the largest pyramid in the world is in Mexico; not in the much talked of region of Yucatan but within a hundred miles of Mexico City—that among the ancient monuments there is a conical "pyramid"—that there is an old city which was covered by a lava flow, and that excavation of it proceeded only far enough to disclose its existence and then slowed down and stopped (in that habit of postponement that so often prevails in tropic countries)—that other extensive ruins very near Mexico City await exploration?

What countless studies of the human race and its history remain untouched, in spite of all that has been done— —desert canyons, Mexican highlands, South American mountains, Bering Sea islands, Greenland, Egypt, Mesopotamia, Arabia, western China, and I suppose a hundred other regions!

MESSENGER BOY

I saw a messenger boy sitting on a stone curbing of the esplanade in front of the New York Public Library. Heaven knows what messages he had with him to deliver! Possibly he was off duty, or out for lunch, but I think not. I think that he had a telegram with him giving instructions for the purchase or sale of a quantity of stocks (immediate—no delay), or a message to the president of some big corporation.

He sat on the curb, and the world of momentous affairs was nowhere in his head. His hat was pushed back and a brush of rusty red hair stuck out from under its visor. He had a large paper bag on his knee, steadied in the hollow of his arm. Crowded together on the stone flagging at his feet were at least one hundred pigeons, all milling around. Under their feet was a carpet of cracked corn, which was being renewed so fast from the paper bag that they couldn't keep up with the supply and they were all excited because of this. The boy was completely unaware, I am certain, that people were stopping to look at him or that traffic was rushing by behind his back. The world consisted exclusively of pigeons.

Of course he will come to a bad end. Responsibility was not in him. Thoughts as to his job had evaporated. He was a complete object lesson in what a young man should not do.

But honestly, I liked him better than certain employees of the library whom I talked with presently, and I know that he was having a better time than an executive in a corporation whom I called on an hour later. Also I surmise that he'd spent a day's wages for the bag of cracked corn.

PROVENDER

I think that there must be squirrel ancestry somewhere in my makeup. When I walked into the South Station a little while ago I stopped in a sort of delight before a store window. Bags of pecans were displayed there; nice, bulging, burlap bags. One, lying on its side, was cut open, and the burlap flaps were turned back, exhibiting a great quantity of smooth, light-brown nuts. I could easily think of myself as an eager and gratified squirrel at work on the contents of that bag, carrying off those nuts one by one and hiding them in a private store somewhere. I could imagine myself chiseling into the shell of a nut now and then and enjoying its meaty contents.

If I were going to be transformed into some smaller and lesser animal, I'd prefer to be a creature that could find an excellent living in nuts, and perhaps in aromatic roots and in seeds from pine cones or from beech trees. I would lay up stocks of these long-keeping foods, and then I would feel all in proper order, ready for whatever might happen. I think that the feeling would be one of great comfort.

AH, TREE!

Let me lean my length
Against thy trunk, for strength.
Let thy form impart
The echo of thy heart.

Let me lift my eyes,
And there against the skies
Let me find outlined
Young leaves on boughs entwined.

Let thy roots that crest
The ground whereon I rest
Give in part to me
The strength they give to thee.

GASPÉ CHILDREN

Today, in this remote part of French Canada where I am staying, I met a delightful group. I was taking a walk on a back road which climbs and climbs up a hill when I heard them coming above me. They were racing down a steep part of the road, largely out of sight behind a rail fence. Then they crossed into a pasture and came at full speed down its stony slope. They stopped on the farther side of a fence opposite me—and we exchanged greetings.

There was first a small boy, perhaps eight or nine years old, second a somewhat smaller girl, third a still smaller, little girl, and fourth a still smaller dog. Attached to the dog was a diminutive cart with two tiny, home-made wheels of solid wood. In the cart was a tin pail and inside of that another. This outfit the small dog brought down the steep, rocky pasture with entire success, he and his companions on a dead run. They went along presently in the direction of the village.

Hardy, smiling, fresh-faced, quiet, eager-eyed youngsters! What a healthful, simple, normal life they lead! Not one of the group, in all probability, has ever seen a motion picture. There is none within a hundred miles. Not one has heard a radio. Not one, probably, stays indoors longer than the time necessary for sleep and for school. Everywhere they are playing outdoors all the time, or busy at such duties as children can do. I doubt if they have ever heard a telephone, for the nearest one is many miles distant.

But these youngsters are not ignorant. They go to school—and besides that they have their own store of knowledge gained in their own place and manner of life. They can teach a dog to haul a cart at top speed down a steep and rocky hill, and they can keep up with the dog without falling and without tiring.

They are not poor in body, mind, or spirit.

Baby swallows now perch upon a low-hanging wire near my cabin. They are the most extraordinary combination of extreme youth and skillful proficiency. They are so young and downy that their feathers make a fuzzy aura around their bodies. Their beaks are very yellow, their shoulders are disproportionately wide, and their wings droop and look much too large for their bodies. They sit close together, as close as they can possibly manage, as if needing the reassurance of another near by. They look at me in baby innocence as I stand a few feet from them.

But they launch out from that wire in strong, beautiful flight— not in long, sustained, ten-minute wheels aloft but in shorter ventures that nevertheless are smooth perfection. This morning a strong, gusty wind was blowing that almost dislodged them from their wire and made them sway alarmingly—but they took off in the teeth of it and made little circles and loops and poises, and came back smoothly to their jerky perch. Once in the air their wings functioned instantly in effective rhythm, meeting the swirling wind at precisely the right angle and with exactly the correct fraction of power, and their small bodies turned and balanced smoothly and gracefully in the perfection of motion.

Yet I suppose that no more than three or four days can have elapsed since they left the nest.

POND LILIES

Yellow pond lilies have raised their heads now many inches above the water in my pond, and there are whole companies of them. True enough, they cannot compare in beauty with the exquisite white lilies, and yet there is something about them that gives them an earned place in a quiet, muddy body of water like mine.

I did not know until I read it in a flower book that the "petals" are not petals at all but sepals.

Isn't it interesting to find this less-beautiful flower raising its head well above the water whereas the luxurious white lily rests at ease—elaborate, confident ease—on the surface? The white lily does not need to stand erect and conspicuous. It can afford to be indolent. In fact, I should say that standing forth in sprightly fashion would be for it just a bit undignified.

THY VOICE

Fling about my shoulders
Gauze from thin moonbeams.
Wrap about my body
Silver from the streams.

Place upon my forehead
Garlands from the fields.
Touch me with the perfume
Purple Iris yields.
Take me where the laughter
Of thy voice will be
Solitary music
Echoed back to me.

IMPRESSIONISM

As I drove to town yesterday morning the lakes and ponds were all smoking with soft, white mist. In one lowland place I saw two cranes mirrored on the small bit of water in which they were standing. They seemed for a moment (gray against the white mist) as though they were part of a Japanese screen from the hands of a true artist. It was an exquisite bit of impressionism.

GLACIER PARK

I have been considering what it is that constitutes the attraction of these mountains in the Glacier Park region. That they are supremely magnificent, gorgeous, inspiring, is unquestionable. Their lines and masses, their pinnacles, their glaciers, their vertical walls—all these make one want to drink in their beauty with long and repeated draughts. They make one wish to see them from every angle and under every circumstance of cloud and light, sunshine and storm. They are an utter spectacle.

They do not invite me to climb to their summits. I know that many of those summits I could not accomplish anyway—but I do not particularly wish to climb them. I should rather stand and look at them.

The isolation and untouched freshness of their valleys appeal strongly. The grass of their mountain meadows is untrod, their flowers unpicked, their streams unsoiled. They are as fresh as creation. To me the greatest delight would be to seek out these valleys, one by one, quietly, without hurry, without schedule, entering each as an adventure in finding and tasting a new world, leaving it just as it is, passing on to other new and inspiring worlds. I think that I should be as much interested in a rock that I could hold in my hand as in a whole crag or summit, as much in a quiet bend in a stream as in a high falls, as much in a trusting gopher as in a band of sheep.

I should want to let the views of magnificent heights be spaced in the midst of other enjoyments. It seems to me that to do other than that would be to tire mind and body, and in the end to dull the thrill and inspiration that otherwise would be so great. And so the existence of valleys and their streams, of gophers and marmots, of birds and flowers and mountain meadows, seems to me a very essential part of the beauty and worth of this region.

APPLE TREE

I am sure that an apple tree needs dead limbs and twigs. It does not *look* like a well-cared-for tree, of course. Nevertheless, I like this one in front of my cabin to be as it is. The small birds—chickadees, sparrows, finches—like the dead twigs better than the live ones. They travel about from one pleasant perch to another, they can see all about, they can choose any one of fifty twigs on which to rest while watching for insects or while singing their songs.

Then its trunk too is interesting. It is not a smooth, well-shaped perfect trunk. It is shaggy, and there is a big cavity in it, and there are openings into this cavity. A chipmunk owns these openings. They are his upstairs doors. He comes out of one, takes his seat on an old stub of a branch, retires into another, reappears somewhere else, and in general gives every evidence of considering the tree excellent and suitable.

Even a dead branch that has fallen from the tree and lies in the grass beneath it belongs where it is. Its twigs, bare and inviting, stand just above the top of the grass and weeds. Birds are continually perching there. I am sure that they find this place attractive in its own way—near the earth and its low vegetation and yet above it where one can see all about.

CHIPMUNK

Do you thrill to the final gay little jump of a chipmunk as he reaches the other side of the road, after crossing it in wise haste? I do. Each time one runs before me in this fashion I find myself waiting for that final "note."

And the tail of a chipmunk, as he hurries along—is it not the most erect bit of dignity ever contrived? It reminds me of the Big Trees because it has an untrembling air about it. I am sure that there is some kinship between this important part of the small creature's body and a giant redwood.

AGING SUMMER

My little pond has reached its full tide of midsummer. Everything about it seems to be resting, as if its urgent mission had been accomplished, and now it could pause and remain quiet for a time.

All of the trees and bushes along its margin have finished the task of growing new twigs and expanding new leaves. The baby needles on pines have lengthened and matured. Alders and maples have taken on the hue of full growth. Cattails are at complete stature, and their brown and compact seed masses are very round. Sedges have thrown out a tangled, green-brown cluster at their summits. The surface of the pond is all spattered with the flat leaves of the yellow pond lily. The blossoms themselves have matured and only latecomers lift their globes above the water. Grasses along the margin are no longer a vivid green but look as if their eager youth had settled down into the quiet, bronze cast of middle age.

The air was still this evening and the pond was unruffled. Two dragon flies wheeled steadily back and forth above its surface. Fifty feet overhead two or three swifts flew in broad curves with rapid wings. Sounds were subdued. From the bordering woods came an occasional, soft bird note that was not a sustained song but was like a contented expression of work done, dangers safely met, children happily started on their way. It seemed as if the birds were speaking to one another in bird voices and saying "All is well." Even the moon, a silver half-disk in the sky, was turned to gold in the water's reflection, as if its white metal were mellowed by the pond's influence. And where, two months ago, my ears caught the shrill, ecstatic peep-peep of the little frogs, I could hear tonight only an occasional meditative, deeply twanging note from the throat of some half-sleepy old fellow, perhaps grown corpulent in the opulence of mid-summer.

My pond conveyed no sense of that which is lifeless. It simply had mellowed. Where earlier it was eager for it knew not what, now it rested in attainment. All of its company had striven to people the earth with their own kind—lilies and cattails, thrushes and frogs, alders and pines—and all had succeeded to the utmost of their ability. Now they and their new generations were resting together.

TO A WOOD LILY

Thou wer't so silent!
Had the sunlight failed to fall
Upon thy drooping head I should
Have found thee not at all.
Thy beauty would have lost its gleam,
There in silent loneliness
Beside the swift, indifferent stream.

Thy face was drooping,
So before thy feet I knelt
To meet thy shy embarrassment.
With tenderness I felt
Thy trembling anthers' dusty tips.
I felt their softness—then I touched
Thy smooth corolla with my lips.

The aspen leaves are all a-twinkle this morning. I can see them from where I sit, and I like to watch their blithe movement against the sky, to hear their patter as of rain.

A frail, short-lived tree of soft wood! Is it not impressive to learn that of all the many kinds of deciduous trees—the oaks and maples and all the rest—the aspen is the very oldest in plant history? Botanists say that it was the first to appear among the deciduous forms of early ages.

WOODCHUCKS

A few days ago, in the little woods back of my cabin, I came upon a dry knoll where woodchucks had almost a town. There were burrows all about. No doubt it is a place where digging is easy and where homes underground remain dry and comfortable. Presently I crossed another knoll in another part of the woods, and found there a second community. I wonder if the two sets of inhabitants visit one another's houses. Possibly they are related—at least by marriage.

What is it, do you suppose, that constitutes special attraction among woodchucks? Who is the popular debutante, and why? Especially soft fur? A fascinating eye? A particularly rich, brown-and-grey color? An especially nice chucky odor? Or other and more "practical" qualities?—perhaps a knowledge as to where fresh clover can be obtained, or a dowry of an excellent abandoned burrow, or a frugal disposition, capable of taking good care of woodchuck finances, or a sound home instinct that offers no danger of wandering off to other woodchuck towns.

And think of all the other small residents of these wooded acres— of the qualities that must define one from another in their own world. How little we know of it all! Surely a certain whitefoot mouse is not merely *any* mouse to others of his kind. In some way— not necessarily at all such as we could understand—he must be *a* whitefoot mouse, an individual, a definite specific creature, recognizable in some hidden way that may be dim to our eyes and yet very definite to other tiny eyes and ears and noses and whiskery faces.

What an exceedingly small fraction of all this we can comprehend, and yet what a world of its own it must be!

CONCEALED WORLD

Last night I stood on the shore of my pond. Its surface was completely motionless, lighted by the half-moon and by a dusky glow from the sun that was far below the western horizon.

It seemed to me that the surface was the most baffling, unrevealing mirror that I could imagine. It showed me sky and clouds. But it concealed a world. Beneath it, I know, lay a region which I could not enter or look into. I know that in that world an intricate life goes on. I know that there are forests of water-plants, that in the midst of these move a host of creatures, busy about their own affairs, seeking their food, fighting their battles, mating, raising their young. An animated, purposeful world! But the mirror of the pond conceals it all. It gives back only the sky and the clouds and the bordering trees.

EAGERNESS

I left the hushed and sleeping world behind
To see what nighttime wonder I could find,
And lo! I caught an eager wisp of dawn
At play, a wayward child, upon my lawn.

FLOWERS

Yesterday and the day before, in the oppressive heat, I went to the pasture and picked daisies, buttercups, paint brush, and self-heal. I came back to the cabin exhausted by the relentless sun and placed those flowers listlessly in a copper bowl. Throughout the day they remained, a monument to my indifference. There was no beauty in them, for I had allowed no softness to enter into my arrangement. They were no joy to me, and although they were unfaded this morning I brutally threw them away.

Today I went to walk in the mist, along a wood road (what a glorious adventure that is at this season of the year!) and I returned later to my cabin with meadow rue, white, soft, feathery, and with yellow loosestrife, delicately dignified as to its golden racemes. *These* I put in my copper bowl, and I put them there with joy and in appreciation of their own beauty. They have been there since morning, and a thousand times I have looked at them with thirsty pleasure.

After this when I cannot spiritually rise to the level of the flowers I seek I shall leave them to grow in the fields.

LAKE ONTARIO

Last night I saw some wild geese on the shore of Lake Ontario. A white goose drifted gently before her retinue of twelve young ones. They were of various shades of soft gray brown. There was so much beauty, so much poetry, in their forms and in their movement that I was quietly and silently enthralled.

NEGRO BEGGAR

Downtown in New York, in that crowded financial region, I saw a negro sitting on the sidewalk. He leaned lightly against a fire hydrant. He had tremendously strong shoulders and chest, but both legs had been removed close to his body. I never saw anyone who so fully represented strength made impotent.

I had passed him while seeing this, and I turned back, feeling in my pocket for money. Somehow that man and his thwarted body seemed utter tragedy.

The negro was not looking up at the people, or saying anything. Perhaps an officer would arrest him if he did. I don't know. Anyway he wasn't doing that. He just sat still. There was a small box on the sidewalk in front of him, and when I stopped I said to him, "What have you got in that box?" He looked up quickly and said "Nothin', boss! I ain't got nothin'!" His face was responsive, and his voice had the quality of a man who joins with you in amusement at his own situation. I don't know what he thought as to why I'd asked. Maybe the box was a beggar's invitation. Maybe it once held things to sell. All I know is that the voice and face were not whining, not cringing, not apologetic.

I gave him a coin, and he thanked me in a way that made me glad that I'd stopped.

ANIMATED FOOD

Aren't you glad that our food does not wriggle before our eyes?

This morning I saw a robin catching his early worm. It was a terrifically animated meal. It expanded and contracted and flung itself about, until my own inner anatomy felt uneasy. The robin did not seem to mind. Then there was a sparrow, the other day, with a fluttering moth. Truly I breathed a prayer of thankfulness that my meat, fish, and other edibles are always well changed from their original animated forms before they come to me.

PHEASANT

What merit have I gained
That I, in dumb
And humble gratitude,
May toss a crumb
Before thy feet
And find thee unafraid,
Unthinking of retreat?

AN AUGUSTUS JOHN

I have been thinking all day with a definite ache of a cool and quiet nook in the Modern Art Museum in Dublin, Ireland. It seems to me that the world would be all that I could wish if I could spend just one more hour there—today.

I want to look a long time upon a Lavery or an Augustus John or the work of some other of those glorious people of our own day who have the divine gift and have captured in color the form and spirit of some bit of beauty.

TEMPERAMENTAL

A fitful rain today, sometimes making little streams on my windowpane, again giving 'way to bright sunshine. It is the sort of rain I particularly like. There is nothing dull and monotonous about it. It is all temperamental, playful, and in its own way winning.

ONCE MORE

Perhaps I'll hear the night-wind
When it sweeps across the sands
And presses down the beach grass
With its soft and trembling hands.

Perhaps I'll see the night-sky
With its island clouds of bliss
Bestow its softness waveward
In a tender moonlit kiss.

Perhaps I'll feel a night-sprite
In its elfin dance of glee
Breathe fast with joyous laughter
As she brushes close to me.

Perhaps, for I'm returning
Where I found them once before,
When the lovely night was falling
On a strange and lonely shore.

DEMEANOR

I do not doubt that even a crow has some sort of quiet, gentle expression that he utters at times—to his wife, for instance, when she is sitting on her nest, or to his new fledglings. He may then be the most considerate lover in the world, by contrast. But I should like to hear that sound some time, just to make up for all the vituperation and hoodlum noises that mark his demeanor the rest of the time.

What is it that develops such definite and varied dispositions in various kinds of animals—not merely in the individual but in the whole group?

At my cabin I watched a red squirrel trying to extricate a piece of suet that was tightly fastened beneath a wire encircling the trunk of a tree. He grabbed it and yanked this way and that. His back fairly quivered with his intensity. He jumped around on the tree trunk, and his manner was one of testy irritation. He acted as if the thing were a personal affront. He grew more and more intent and testy with each yank.

All red squirrels, it seems to me, are short-tempered, and easily become querulous. Why? What in their race-history or habits or food or whatnot has made them this way?

Dogs are affable. Coyotes are unapproachable. Yet they are related. Hunters declare that a rhinoceros is quick-tempered and quarrelsome. A lion is good-tempered—a swash-buckler, but not constantly looking for trouble, as does the rhinoceros. Think of the otter—easily tamed by a man who knows how, likeable and friendly when confined, even capable of following his owner around, as does a dog. On the other hand a mink never relaxes from his bitter ferocity, no matter how close his association with man.

Every kind of animal, big and little, seems to have its own kind of disposition. Wouldn't it be interesting if we could know all the circumstances and all the history that brought this about!

I wish that we knew more about it.

CHURCH·SUPPERS

Whenever I am a guest at a supper served in a church—you know, where each woman contributes something that she has prepared, a cake or a pie or a salad, each one different from all the rest, some of them thick and some thin, some elaborate and some a bit sad—I have a feeling as if I were prying into the domestic affairs of the contributors. It seems to me that the very successful cake is a little surrounded with a halo of self-satisfaction or at least self-congratulation, and the thin or lop-sided or fallen one is an unhappy and unfortunate advertisement of hard luck.

All of them give me the feeling that they really belong in the privacy of their owners' homes, and that I have no business to be looking them over, as if I were peeping through the kitchen window.

IN THE MIDST OF CONFLICTS

In the midst of all the troubles and conflicts of the human race, something deeply reassuring comes to me when I look out upon the steadfast outdoor world—the woods and hills, meadows and plains. I had that feeling last week in driving through the hills of southern Indiana and Ohio. I feel it in the untouched parts of New England. It has come to me strongly in those great regions of the West.

I am not thinking merely of the fact that in the fields human beings can raise food and make a living. What I mean is something deeper than that. It is the unshakable foundation of sanity and rightness that the whole outdoor world in itself represents. This is what gives me the feeling of reassurance as I look out upon it. No matter in what difficulties man may involve himself, in his personal affairs or in all the complexities of civilization, he still has within reach this unswerving open world that does not change.

The pines and all their kindred are not going to alter their ways and start off on some new and hasty and ill advised course. The moccasin flowers will continue in their beauty. The sparkle of sunlight on the ripples in a stream is not going to become something different and less desirable. Even though all these things are very intricate in their adjustment of one part to another, they are also dependable. Thousands of centuries have been occupied in bringing them into being, and they will go on.

Sometimes the cities and towns and all the artificial things appear to be discouragingly wide-spread. It seems difficult to get away from them. But they are still only a tiny fraction. I do not know how large a fraction, but it must be very small. No matter if one must live under their conditions, no matter if so much of the human race lives in these surroundings, the background of the unchanging open world is not far away. Its secure and ordered course goes on, and will continue.

VALIANCY

I'd rather be a wind-torn tree,
Gaunt and brave at timberline,
Or crouching by a hostile sea,
Than one that's nurtured, husbanded,
Until from root and formal bough
That spark of valiancy has fled
That is the soul of trees that stand
Beneath the stars—against the storms—
Their roots in soil-impoverished land.

PREPARATIONS FOR SLEEP

How closely our ways parallel those of the lesser creatures!

Last week I watched a large and varied company of birds in a zoological garden, composing themselves for the night. True, they were in an enclosure—but it was so extensive that it was almost like a free world. A tall tree grew within it. A stream ran through it, broadening into a shallow pond.

Dusk was coming on, and evidently it was time to settle down and go to sleep. But the performance might just as well have been that of an equal number of human beings in some big dormitory. There were restless individuals and those who were quiet or wanted to be, noisy specimens and those who made no sound, peaceable birds and petulant, nuisances and good fellows.

At least a third of the colony occupied an unconscionable length of time merely in arranging their feathers, and for some reason these were mostly the large birds or the homely. They stretched first one wing and then the other. They flapped both wings for long periods, not enough to raise their bodies but quite enough to disturb their neighbors. With long beaks they combed each feather interminably.

A big bird on a branch of the tree could not find precisely the position that suited him. He would move a few inches this way and that. His neighbors had settled down and evidently had gone to sleep. Seemingly this fact irritated him. Suddenly he stood up, and flapped across, dislodging his nearest neighbor, and occupying, himself, the space made vacant.

Meanwhile two gulls on the ground started a quarrel. Their voices rose. One of them flew to another part of the enclosure, arousing and scattering a number of birds there. The second followed and the quarrel was continued. Finally, in a sort of sleepy diminuendo, it died down.

When it was almost dark a big bird, still awake, apparently decided that a late bath would be desirable. He went down to the pool, walked in, stayed for a minute or two, came out, and returned to the region where his interrupted preparations for the night had been started. Another bird of another kind started to copy this performance, went as far as the margin of the pool, but lost enthusiasm and came back without entering the water.

It was all extraordinarily human.

I LOVE MY TOWN AT DAWN

I love my town at dawn,
When the eastern sky's afire,
When shadows, touched with rose,
Caress each slender spire,
When glints of golden light
From a distant skyland plain
Find laughing rest at last
Upon each window pane.
I love its river path

When the water-birds take wing,
And rise o'er old roof tops
Toward clouds where dawn winds sing.
And then the winding streets
As the night light drifts away,
I love their stones—so still—
So moist with dew—so grey.
I love my town at dawn
When I hear its first dim sigh
As it rises from its sleep
And bids the stars "Good-bye."

WATER STRIDER

The water-striders must be making ready for their winter's sleep. They all, so far as known, spend the winter under protecting material, leaves, grass, debris of some sort—beneath the banks, or maybe down at the bottom of the pool.

There are many species, but all depend on the surface tension of the water to support them. Some at least have a coating of very short, thick-growing hairs. The coating on their legs and feet rests on the surface film of the water.

CHANCE SUNLIGHT

Last week I was looking out of a window at my cabin. I saw a slender, horizontal branch of maple leaves that seemed to float in the air because the rest of the tree was out of view. Its background was a group of slender tree-trunks. I saw it because a chance ray of sunlight illuminated it at that moment. It was a beautiful, graceful thing, and having once discovered it, I found that I could return to it and enjoy it, again and again.

PERSONAL MOON

A great yellow moon in the morning sky this morning, giving pale light to the marshes, a soothing touch to the heart.

The dawn moon is personal. More so than one in the night sky. I am glad this day began with such beautiful and intimate mystery.

DARKNESS

The gift of darkness!—the darkness of night and the open sky! I think that we do not enjoy it enough, do not seek as much as we might its beauty and its healing rest.

Away back before the beginnings of history, the coming of night must have meant for many creatures relaxation from their activities of day. While the sun shone food must be sought and all of the work of living must be pursued. Then came the slow quenching of sunlight and all that goes with it. Then came darkness—stars—quiet—and I think that with this was meant to come a sort of sharing in the inner character of a world lighted only by the distant stars, a composing of the body to the tempo of night. For man himself there could come also a spiritual sharing, an attunement to the quiet and beauty of darkness.

But everywhere and forever we shatter the dimness of night. In cities and towns we must have our way lighted, the more brilliantly the better. Inside the walls of our homes we do the same. Wherever we go we demand illumination, and the nearer it can approach to daylight the more we speak of it with pride. Not until we are ready to close our eyes in sleep do we permit darkness, and if sleep comes slowly we are fretful and demand light. If we are outdoors in darkness we must have light in order that we may hurry to some place where there is light.

I think that we are missing one of the joys of life. I think that we might well seek that joy more frequently, and that we would be the better for the seeking.

TO A FALLING STAR

In haste and out of this far night
You fall, while all the rest remain.
The silent loneness of your flight!
Majestic!—but as if your reign
Had reached its end, as if the hour
Of banishment, in swift surprise
Had robbed you of your power
And hurled you crownless from the skies.

FROM A PHANTOM MEMORY

How soft thy steps—how dim!
Their falling faintly beats upon my ear!
How far away thou art—
And yet—my Love—thou'rt near.

Mere ghostly footsteps thine,
Shadows from a phantom memory.
Yet—thou art by my side
And—bending down to me!

THREE ABREAST

The other day, on a city street, I saw something that gave me a thrill. It was a heavy dray drawn by three great big matched horses moving abreast.

Ever since I can remember, this combination of horses has given me a delightful feeling bordering on awe. It has always signified luxurious power, a richness of possessions in the way of stalwart horse-flesh and a determined disposition in the management of an unusual arrangement of lines and traces. I can remember such teams as far back as I can remember anything.

Always I have looked at the three horses searchingly and never have I found any one of them different from the others. By some secret miracle they are precisely alike. They move, too, with the same step, and with an even front. No one of the three is a leader. They have a complete unity of purpose and method.

Once in a long while I have seen such a team attached to a dray the floor of which was built on a curve, rising higher in front and sloping toward the ground at the rear. This makes the whole affair doubly interesting. Only very heavy freight of a very special kind could require such a dray or indeed could remain in place on it. To own and use such a conveyance signifies originality and the same fearless purposefulness indicated by the driving of three horses abreast.

Horses in pairs have always seemed to me an excellent institution—but ordinary. Horses in sequence of pairs have meant circuses—and therefore something from a fanciful and unreal world, or else a tallyho and quite outside my personal realm. Horses three abreast are real, impressive, significant.

No motor truck, no matter what its capacity in tons and no matter what its rated horse-power or its speed, can ever equal the three horses. A truck is just a factory product, efficient but uninspired.

WHAT JOY IS THEIRS?

What joy is theirs, those creatures living deep in shells,
The tortoise and the shellfish by the sea?
Do sunlight and the swift wind mean to them
As much as they have always meant to me?

Does trouble ever cloud their way and make it bleak,
And do they bask in real and conscious bliss?
If I could speak the language that they speak,
I'd ask, and hope that they would tell me this.

BALLET

Small, individual, swiftly moving, white clouds crossing the deep night-sky in the early hours this morning. They were all of the same size, moving along before the same swift night-wind, and in their own way they were filled with femininity and grace. I watched them, and it seemed as though I were watching a ballet—a

ballet that held nothing of modernism and angularities in its rhythm, but was all soft and white and ethereal—a ballet amid the stars, dancing away into the distance and beyond the path of the moonlight.

BRAHMS

Last night I listened to a Brahms sonata—a sonata in C Minor—played by someone who understood.

With the first few notes there came into being a stream that flowed brightly through dim woods, emerging now and then to pass between unshaded banks, falling a little to curve through a great, wide plain where sunset gave wine shades to water and grasses, flowing along lazily for a while, and then on to lower lands where it fled rapidly through the night to some far-off sea.

THE BUSY MAN

I wonder if anywhere in the world among busy men—men who are carrying multiple, pressing responsibilities—there exists one who does not feel sometimes an overwhelming desire to get away from it all, to find refuge in some simpler mode of existence.

Perhaps there are men who never feel this. Perhaps for some it is completely satisfactory to clip the minutes all day, every day, and always to reach the end of a day with a sense of unfulfilled obligations. Some men *seem* to be made that way.

But I suspect them. They are stimulated by manifold endeavor. They give the *impression* of complete sufficiency. Most of the time they give this to themselves. They would even argue the merits of their programs. But I suspect them.

Now and then some hard-pressed executive makes a confession to me, in a moment of reaction. His whole attitude changes. He becomes wistful, yearning. Usually what he wants is something utterly simple to secure, you'd think—nothing more than a chance to put on old clothes, putter around a cabin or a camp-fire, just to do completely simple things.

But of course what he really wants is not easy at all. He wants not merely to do those things but to bring to them an unencumbered mind and body and spirit, not merely to escape from his crowded daily schedule but to escape from all that lies behind and in and ahead of it. And that is no simple matter for any man.

Honestly, men and their work are a mystery!—to their friends, to the chance observer, to themselves.

I wonder why?

I wonder if the only wise man may not be he who has the courage to cut straight through to the heart of things and to do what he really longs to do, to seek the goal in which, inwardly, he believes.

I wonder if the very greatest need in the education of young folk may not be to convey to them in some way a vastly clearer and more authentic understanding of human values.

I wonder if a new Socrates, who would teach enduring values—not sentiment, nor business psychology, nor pessimism, nor even religious fervor—may not be needed quite as much today as in ancient Greece.

I wonder how he could ever make himself heard—until his hearers were too old to make much use of his urgings.

And I wonder if this same question in all its urgency has not existed in some similar form for a considerable number of thousands of years—?

A CHINESE SCREEN

An island by a winter sea—
Rimmed with frosted spume;
A drooping, flowering wild plum tree,
By a sea sprite's tomb;
A mouse-skin bat with pinioned wings,
Poised in soft, gray flight;
A brush-stroke harmony that brings
Infinite delight!

OLD FARMHOUSE

Each time that I drive over the road that leads southwest from my town I pass an old farmhouse, a big old place, that has never in all its life seen a coat of paint. Its clapboards are just the color of the bark of the trees that surround it, just the shade of the stones in the walls near by. I am certain that when it was built, perhaps two hundred years ago, its walls were left just as they were, have remained untouched ever since.

Somehow there is a certain peacefulness in the appearance of the old house. There is a sort of restfulness in its looks. It is at the opposite pole from the alertness of the well-trimmed, sprucely painted house. It seems to speak a different philosophy.

A DAWNING THAT SINGS

Sleep—lead me yonder where dream flowers bloom,
Mid fairy-pink heather and pale yellow broom,
Where frail florets blossom—where colors are bright,
Where soft, folding petals make ready for night.
Lead me—I pray thee—where dream creatures roam—
Find me a satyr—a fun-loving gnome.
Take from my memory all mournful things,
Bring to my spirit a dawning that sings.

BEWITCHING MOMENT

This morning, high in the sky, a soft dim sky, the waning crescent moon. A few stars were in attendance. All sorts of words drifted in and out of my mind as I stood there and watched—words such as "unknown," "glory," and others. It was an alluring, bewitching moment, and I drained it of all that it had to give.

FROM DARKNESS

As some Cimmerian soul—alone and brave—
Ventures forth from his beshadowed cave
To meet an unknown dawn,
So do I with unaccustomed eyes
Venture forth and, looking fearlessly above,
Behold the vast effulgence of thy love.

ICE SPIRES

I had just been reading a clipping about "ice spires," and within the hour, beside a country road, I found beautiful ice crystals. Here and there, in a few spots, I saw grass stems or pieces of leaves or twigs, recumbent in sheltered places, that bore exquisite fronds and plates and plumes of frail, feathery, branching, white crystals. I did not have a hand lens with me, but I am sure that their forms were intricate and beautiful.

One slender twig was decked with plumes at least an inch and a half long, a solid row of them on each side. It was like a giant feather dropped by some white bird from the far North. I picked that one up carefully and carried it back with me, trying not to jar it and lose its adornment. It is now deposited in a sheltered spot under a pine tree back of my office. Perhaps I shall be able to make a photograph of it tomorrow.

115

If there is one prayer that I would utter above all others, one gift that I would ask for myself and for every human being, now and for all time, it is this—

Let me have faith.

Not merely the faith that looks to such limited visions as I can summon out of my own imperfect imaginings—

Not merely the faith that would rely on my inadequate reasoning—

But faith in the integrity of the pattern of all life, in the ultimate rightness of that pattern, in its inevitable completeness, in its immeasurable beauty.

Let me remember that never in all the world can any human mind comprehend, or even glimpse, more than the smallest fraction of all the elements that enter into any least part of that pattern.

Let me continuously remember that not one exquisite curve in a bird's wing, not one gentle intonation in a human voice, not one heroic deed, not one renunciation, could have come about except as the result of countless forces and contacts and events, all interwoven and interacting. Let me find joy and wonder in these things, and let me find an equal joy in the ordered intricacy that has made them what they are.

Let me realize that the complexity that baffles me in my own life and hopes is not disorder, except in my own imperfect vision and understanding.

Give me that faith, and in its incontestable rightness let me walk steadily forward.

LIEBER

I'd like a song to tiptoe where
My thoughts lie deep in sleep,
A song that drifts upon the air
In long and gentle sweep.
A little song, demure and meek,
With laughter that can bring
A darling dimple to its cheek,
A little song that I might sing.
I'd like its breath to still my dreams
With minor lullabies,
And send them off on golden streams,
Adrift across the skies.
And then I'd like to feel it press
Its lips, all moist with dew,
Upon my thoughts—a dear caress
That comes, perhaps, from You!

ENCHANTMENT

Awake and dreaming tonight! I walked upon the ice floes formed by small white clouds. I tiptoed from star to star. I put my cheek to the cool, full moon.

Enchanted by this winter night, you see!

THIRST

If my spirit can not live
Forever on with singing lips,
Forever drinking sparkling sips
Of wonder born from dew-dipped leaves,
From falling stars, from every breath
Of Life, and from the hush of Death,
Let not my spirit slumber on
In bleak content, without a throb
Of flooding ecstacy to rob
The passing hours of paltry sleep!
But let an agony enshroud
Its fragile form in such a cloud
Of bitter gloom that it will seek
To tear apart the pall and slake
A newborn thirst within the wake
Of sunlight as it gives a pawn
Of glory to the breaking dawn!

IMPENDING

Today interests me because of its smoothly hidden intent.

Outside my cabin window the deep snow is grayly indefinite. It is voluminous and all-covering, but it has no clearly defined character, no ripple-marks from wind, no glistening crust. Overhead the sky matches the snow. It is filled with cloud substance, and yet there is no individual cloud in it anywhere. There is no suggestion of wind. The temperature is neither freezing nor thawing but is completely neutral, like the sky and the snow.

The day is not one of foreboding. It is too neutral to be threatening. And yet, deeply concealed in its bones, it seems to have all the makings of far-reaching purpose. It is like a large and gray-furred animal that appears to be peacefully sleeping but has a complete set of claws, withdrawn and concealed, which it may elect to use when it is fully ready—or may not.

By this time tomorrow a new blizzard will be howling, or a warm sun will be melting the snow into deep slush, or a west wind will be piling this gray stuff in new drifts, or a tobogganing temperature will be making my cabin walls and the trees snap with cold.

Something is brewing.

COLOR

The beautiful colors in the glowing coals of a wood fire! I watched mine—swiftly flowing orange tints and lemon yellow, and waves of purple—and I wondered what combination of soil and sap and sunshine and winter cold had brought into being wood that gave these tints. If I knew, perhaps I could raise trees that had the right ingredients. Then they would be certain to yield their last substance to the flowing beauty of color in a fire.

TANTALIZING?

What do you suppose a sunflower seed smells like to a squirrel— or a chickadee? Does it make their mouth water?

"MASTERY OF NATURE"

How completely sufficient unto themselves the elemental forces are, and what trifling progress mankind has made in effectively meeting them! Shelter to live in—yes—but chipmunks and woodchucks and a host of other lowly creatures achieved that several thousand years ago. As for the birds, those that needed to do so merely arranged to avoid winter conditions entirely.

All this that people speak of as man's "mastery of nature"— Mastery? Man really makes no more than the tiniest, invisible dent. Snows come, winds blow, rains fall or fail to fall, the sun shines too hot or too little—and every single human being on all the earth is profoundly and inescapably affected.

I have tremendous respect for the resourcefulness of natural forces. They are not going to be "mastered" by anybody.

What I like to think of is the ability to shape needs and activities to the play of these forces. The little woods creature that makes a snug house under the snow does this. The weed seeds do it in a thousand different ways. A host of insect species do it, both those that live in water and those that live on land. The fish in the streams do it.

Alongside all the books that have been written on the accomplishments of the human race in "subduing" nature, I should like to see a book that describes the extraordinary ways in which lesser living organisms *use* nature. It would have to be the biggest book in all the world.

MIRRORED STARS

Upon a holy hill,
Where dawn is wont to kneel
And worship at the shrine,
Where violet shades at dusk
Take part in rites divine,

There rests a pool that brims
With stars and pure moonlight—
Rich offering from the swift,
Dark pilgrimage of Night!

SOARING ARCHES

What infinite variety of grace and beauty there is in the forms of
our familiar trees, our elms and maples, birches and beeches! When
I look up at their branches against the sky, when I think of their
perfect union of worthy and strong structure and graceful curve
and outline, I feel that my own liking for similar form and structure
in the buildings that man creates is a natural preference—a preference that goes back through the thousands of years that man has
lived in the midst of trees.

After all, an old cathedral with its soaring arches, its buttresses,
its traceries in the stonework of its walls and spires, is closely akin
to the sweeping limbs and branches and leaves of the trees that
man has looked up to for countless centuries, and in which he has
found satisfying beauty.

TO YOU

My Love, no steps lead down.
The castle wall is high.
I see you far below—
To reach you, I must fly.

No wings have I, my Love,
But curb that shall not be.
Like Icarus I'll soar—
Hold out your arms to me!

BROKEN CLOUDS AT SUNSET

A mighty Hand has crushed a wealth of pearls,
Breaking wide the lustrous nacre shells,
So that pale colors, born beneath the sea,
Welling from their broken homes lie free.

A mighty Hand has bared their secret hearts,
Closed 'till now in smooth and gray-white walls,
Has rent apart the shroud of mystery,
Born of windowless opacity.

A mighty Hand has hurled these broken pearls,
Fragments of a treasure doomed to fade,
Aloft—and there where clouds of passion lie
They grace the forehead of the western sky!

UNCALCULATING

Always I have enjoyed the man who likes to "stand up" to his work—to tackle it without too much calculating of the effort it will require, or the net, cold results that it will yield to him. I like to see him swing boldly at it, gaining a part of his reward simply from doing vigorously the thing that's to be done. Admittedly maximum personal gain may not always be achieved in that way. Admittedly cool, long-distance planning may yield the most in temporal reward. Nevertheless I think that there is another kind of merit in just *doing* a thing, wholeheartedly and with vigor, for the sheer sake of doing it, honestly and thoroughly and with pleasure in the doing.

I think, too, that many a worth-while end is reached through that process. One cannot always plan through to the ultimate outcome. If one were to wait always until a satisfactory end could be seen, a lot of good things would never come about.

A NEW RABBIT

Early this morning a furry shape moved dimly about on the snow beneath my window. Mr. Rabbit was lingering until almost daylight to pick up his breakfast. I suppose that the deep, wet snow in the woods made it difficult for him to find enough food there. But what a timid fellow he was! While he nosed around, I saw three or four tree sparrows approaching in their characteristic way, making little zigzagging advances in the midst of the elderberry bushes. Even those tiny creatures seemed to alarm the rabbit. Or maybe it was the growing light. In a few moments he had gone, back to the shelter of the woods.

Why is it that a rabbit has come to depend so completely on running away? Why is he so timid? His strong hind legs show that this has been his habit for unnumbered generations. Many other creatures who are equally defenseless as to fighting equipment seem confident enough and do not hesitate to move about freely in daylight hours. What was it that caused the rabbit to be so timid?

I wish that I might have a confidential conversation with a rabbit some time and persuade him that he need not run away from everything. Then I wish that he might raise a family instructed in self-confidence, and that they might found a line of rabbits that would stand up for their rights.

Wouldn't it astonish the rest of the woods animals if suddenly a rabbit should turn on them!

I'd like to start a rabbit on a career.

CYPRESS

If we ever want to build something that will last for the next several hundred years I think we'd better make it of cypress. Apparently it will not deteriorate much for the next ten or fifteen generations.

RAW FEATHERS

I saw a window display this week that made me feel as if I were looking on something inhuman that ought never be. I had never seen anything like it before. It was on a street where nearly all the stores sell women's hats (wholesale, largely) and trimmings for hats. This window had a sign "Raw Feathers." In the window there were bundles of bird-feathers, and bird wings, and bird skins, tied up in lots like merchandise from a factory. There were sheaves of long, gold and bronze feathers, such as those from the tail of a pheasant, and bundles of shorter, downier feathers, and whole skins of birds—not mounted birds but the flat skins, each with the head attached.

I do not know when I have seen anything that made me sense so fully the hard commercialization that is involved in the selling of beautiful natural objects, where this means taking animated and beautiful life. It seemed as if trade and commerce had stepped over into a realm where merchandising as we know it has no right place. It was like dealing in the desecrated spirit of song and color and blithe motion.

Later I noticed a woman wearing a hat in which there was a single, long, pheasant feather, like those I had seen.

I suppose that there must be trade in all things that people want to buy. And the bird plumage continues to convey beauty for a long period—perhaps to many people. But I felt that the men who conducted the place that I saw must be a callous lot.

READY TO SPEAK

I have been watching Winter give way.

The deep covering of snow that had buried the earth for many weeks has been yielding to forces beyond its control. A short time ago snow-ploughs were fighting it, but could make only narrow lanes in its midst. Nothing that human beings could do got very far with it. But suddenly there came a day of warm south wind, then a day of gentle rain, and then a cloudless warm sun. And the snow had to yield.

This afternoon time I saw the products of the earth, like long-lost messengers. In one place the gray rock face of a granite ledge stood out, free at last from snow and ice. In another the yellow tops of dead weeds lifted their heads above the surrounding white blanket. They were inanimate, lifeless things, but they seemed like something ready to speak. They did not need voices in order that they might tell their story of soil filled with living roots and seeds, ready to spring to life. It seemed to me that the face of the ledge was almost smiling in the sunlight, in its own gray, grim way; that the weed-tops were thrusting the clinging snow away from them impatiently and confidently.

While it lasts, Winter seems possessed of relentless power. But now other forces are teaching it its place.

AWAKE, DEAR SPRING!

Awake, dear Spring, for I am waiting
Where gulls rise o'er the frozen sea,
And I am watching
To see what your first sign will be.

Perhaps, dear Spring, 'twill be the falling
Of one gray feather from the sky,
The careless off'ring
As northbound geese are passing by.

LOVE SONGS

I am listening to parts of Tristan and Isolde, and understanding even more deeply than ever how much love and music belong together. Even the most primitive of all humans, at the very dawn of our beginnings, and at the first consciousness of voice, must have expressed his love emotions in some crude song of his own.

NEARNESS

I have been speeding North from Virginia through a softness and wetness that I like. It pleases me especially today that skies are gray and near at hand overhead, that trees and bushes are dripping, that water stands in many pools in the fields, and that raindrops are making little momentary raised spots all over those pools, with quickly disappearing circles surrounding each spot. The limbs of hardwood trees are dark and wet, and it would take good searching to find dry areas under thick evergreens, though such areas are there.

Nearby objects in meadows and woodlands have their true place in the world today, not overlooked in thought because of bigger and more distant aspects of the scene. Mountains have retired for a time into a misty seclusion, very large and very silent. Simple nearby rocks have become the visible heights on the face of the world. Little streams are the biggest water courses in evidence and therefore rank for a time at the top. That must be pleasant for a stream that is ordinarily termed merely a brook. Woods today have become family groups of individual trees.

I think that the ground underneath trees has new variety and increased interest today. Hollows are more than wet. They are little imitations of ponds. Leaves from last year have become more compacted—one more step in their journey toward the time when they will be the nurturing mothers of new little trees that presently

123

will lift new faces to a new sky. Pine needles have settled down still more closely into one another's company. In the soil bulbs and roots are feeling the stir of coming activity. Perhaps today in some hidden warm and dry burrow a mother chipmunk is sensing beside her the softly stirring bodies of new baby chipmunks.

Tomorrow the air will be clear and will gain again in depth. The mountains and hills will come out from their misty retirement.

THE PLOUGH

I am the onward forging plough,
Offering the gift of toil
To the barren, dormant soil.
Where the weight of Winter's snow
Pressed upon the ground, I go,
Furrowing the sullen field,
Crushing it to clods, that yield,
Turning up the underlayer,
Giving to the young Spring air
That rare essence of rebirth,
Perfume from the moist, black earth.
Now a smooth-rimmed woodchuck hole,
Now the tunnel of a mole,
Falls beneath my ruthless thrust,
Crumbling back to formless dust.
On I go, my way defined,
Onward—ever in my mind
All the deep, impatient need
Of the waiting, eager seed!

SHELTERED

A bare tree against the sky—blue-jays in sharp flight amid the bare limbs—a chill wind—but within my cabin two fires upon two hearths, mellow pine walls all about, and possessions, treasured to the smallest one.

HERALDS

Soon there will be Spring—and birds—and bird-songs—

It always seems to me that a robin or a bluebird singing from a tree-top, or a finch or song-sparrow pouring out its music from a bush, is the essence of buoyant life, a creature that finds the world good and finds living in the world a happy adventure. I wonder if there may not be some such inner background in its song—not definitely felt as such of course, yet of the same nature as the feeling that comes to human beings when they are living their lives in rightness of adjustment and in a freedom to be themselves at their natural best—released from the worries and perplexities that so much of the time beset them and stifle their song.

COMPETITIVE ACTIVITY

I think that for all living creatures a certain competitive activity is wise and healthful. Every bit of development of all life has been based on its good effects. If for any kind of creature it ceases, the results are bound to be harmful, and that kind of creature, I suppose, will no longer exist.

I have a feeling that the right amount of competitive effort is more logically and more fully established for other creatures than it is for man. It seems to me that considerable numbers of human beings have too little of it for their own good, that others have too much, and that those who have just the right amount are pointedly in the minority. I wish that it might be possible for each of us in his own work to see clearly just what the right amount of active, daily effort is, and then somehow to establish that amount as a going arrangement.

But not inviolably! Regardless of the "right," predetermined amount I would not do away with intense, even consuming, activity at the right time and for the right cause. There are human objectives that are worth all the devotion and self sacrifice in the world. To lessen that or to do away with it would be utter loss. The point is that there must be sufficient objective. If *that* is good and right, nothing is too much.

TRANSFORMED BY MIST

The steel mills and coal piles and ore dumps of this country approaching Chicago are all softened and blended this morning in gray and white mist. Smoke plumes merge with the sky, and clouds of steam fade away in the fog. The steel frames of unloading cranes have lost their hard outlines and seem as if lightly floating creations of the moisture and the wind. Even the lines of freight cars on sidings seem like brush-strokes on a tenuous canvas. Stretches of grass and weeds beyond them become the softest of dim backgrounds. A long line of board fence, painted red and bearing large letters in yellow, is so blended and toned that it brings no jarring note, but merges quietly into the whole gray picture.

Thus can millions of tiny drops of water make beautiful that which without them would be ugly.

I HEAR THE BEAT OF THY HEART

I hear the beat of thy heart
In the flood song of reckless streams,
I see thy swift-purposed soul
When the down-flashing lightning gleams,
I feel thy spirit's warm breath
Where the ghost of the desert lies,
And find the touchstone of love
In the shadows within thy eyes.

These last few days everything around me in the world outdoors gives me the feeling that something is going on behind my back—that it has been going on in secret for a number of weeks and is now all planned, plotted, prepared, and ready to break out. It is like sitting blind-fold in a meeting of conspirators.

For months, until a few days ago, the ground has been deeply buried in snow. It is exposed now, and it looks wet and dead, as if it had not begun at all to awaken from its long-continued frozen condition. But is it numb and unawakened? Has it been doing nothing? Something about it makes me suspect it.

The maple trees appear to be precisely as they were in December—bare trunks, bare limbs, bare twigs—no outward sign of inward life. I suspect them too. Willows and alders are brown and gray and dull, lifeless green. I know that one of these days I shall suddenly discover that the long slender twigs of the willows are vivid green, that the alders are hanging out flower catkins. It will seem as if the whole thing had come about overnight. But will that be true? I doubt it.

Last Sunday a bluebird appeared from nowhere and sang from a bare tree-top. Yesterday robins showed up. One moment they were not here, and the next they were on hand—an instant transformation. But I know that they had been on their way for many days.

I think that everything else, too, has been on its way for weeks—the ground, the trees, the bushes, the grass—everything. I cannot see or hear what is going on. It is hidden and secret and concealed. But I sense conspiracy, like the noiseless approach of invisible figures in the black night, and I think that all at once the plot will break.

THE VOID

I dip my fingers in the blue night stream
That lies with slumbering depth amidst the stars.
Outstretched upon an earthbound bank, I dream
And watch white cloud ships pass with silver spars.

I dream and wonder from what voiceless pool
The stream has come, and where its delta hides,
And if its silent passing leaves a cool
Caress upon the star cliffs' molten sides.

LOGS

I cannot get used to seeing a motor truck tearing along the highway with a load of logs, fresh from the forest. Sawed lumber is different. Boards and squared timbers are a manufactured product, and I feel that a truck has a right to haul them and to make as much speed about it as it chooses. But logs, with all their beauty of bark and form—logs that only a few hours before were the living, upright trunks of big trees—these should not be hustled off to a mill in such fashion.

When a load passes me, whizzing along at thirty or forty miles an hour, I have a feeling of dismay. The thing seems incongruous. I want to stop the truck and ask its driver to proceed more slowly and with more regard for his burden. Better still, I'd like to see the gasoline engine break down or a tire blow out.

When horses haul logs there is some sort of fair contest. If the load is a large one—as most lumbermen arrange that it shall be—the logs have a way of their own. They are capable of starting off in a direction not intended by the driver, and fetching up against an obstruction that ends matters for a time. If the route lies down-hill they may embark on a wild and rather splendid career. If they are to be hauled up-hill, the load must be greatly reduced, so that those remaining may be unable to hold back successfully. In any case, progress is seemly and decent.

With a motor truck, the whole affair is unseemly and indecent.

MATING

Ride with the wind, small bird!
Feel on thy underwing
Rapture, the surge of Spring.
Let thyself be hurled
High o'er the budding world.
Meet thy mate in the sky,
Riding the wind-waves' crest,
Conscious of eager quest.
Race with thy rich voice mute,
Swiftly in sure pursuit.
Capture her on the wing!
Rest then, small bird—and sing!

DESERT

Such desert places as I have visited have been well worth the acquaintance. I admire the plants that grow there. True, they have no luxuriousness, no gentleness, no softness. There is no mildness in their nature. They are not inviting. They hold out no welcoming hand, as do the wild flowers and shrubs, the ferns and mosses, of eastern woods and meadows. But they are resolute and strong. Bitter stem and sap, leaves turned edgewise to the hot sun, tough stems that serve in place of leaves, thick and impervious surface, roots that extend for many yards, coats of barbed spines— all these they utilize. They have learned their hard lesson, have

profited by their experience, and have fought their way against adversity to a secure, impregnable place in the world. They ask no favors, and they need none.

MAKE-BELIEVE

I think that it is wise for us to have a certain amount of make-believe in what we do and think about—a certain amount of pushing the realities away so far that we forget them. There are bound to be realities that are deadening. What we know to be most worth while is not always that which concretely surrounds us, but rather that which we can find in our minds and spirits.

I think that what we need at times, more than anything else, is the opportunity to see and hear and touch, in an almost child-like enjoyment, that which is more than half spiritual and imaginative—the leaves and the tree-trunks against the sunlight—the night sky—music—a tiny tree looking up through the snow—these and a thousand more. It is the spirit of all this that can lift us out of the world of daily living. In the presence of all this, other things lose their power to harm. Other things have place enough at best. We want them to have none at all at times, and I am certain that when that can be, we are the better for it. We are then what each of us is meant to be—more so than we usually find opportunity to be.

Most human beings are never so happy as when that which might be called unreality becomes real. I am sure, beyond any doubt, that in this lies something that is completely fine.

ETERNAL

As moonbeams on yellow grass
Transform the sere and the dead
To throbbing beauty, and pass
Their shafts to the sleeping roots,
So does a love that I know
Come in silence to spread
Through the hollow of winter night
On the spirit of sleeping dead
Karma of golden light.

ROOTS

How well I know the kind of stream that I can see from my car window here in Ohio—

Rich slopes lead down deliberately to the shallow, tree-filled valley through which the stream flows. In some places there are outcroppings of limestone, soft gray, sheered off in vertical cliffs a few yards high, like small replicas of great canyon walls. Sometimes these cliffs rise directly from the water of the stream; sometimes they lie at the border of the small plain that is the floor of the valley. Always they show distinct layers, as clearly marked as the courses of stone in a wall, and always little ferns and vines grow here and there in the crevices where layers meet.

A very mixed company of trees border the stream and lean over it—sycamores with flaking bark and silvery patches, rough-barked elms, strong maples, hackberries that look like elms at a distance, low-growing redbud and dogwood, shaggy hickories, spreading black walnuts. Woodbine and wild grape hang from their branches.

Even though their crowns interlace the ground beneath them is open. You can wander where you will, and in the Spring you can see, unrolled ahead of you, a carpet of anemones and Dutchman's breeches and May-apples and violets. If you reach a space where the trees give way overhead, and if it is mid-summer, you will find weeds growing very tall and thick—horse-weed and black-eyed susans and ironweed.

The stream is shallow for the most part, and it flows alternately over ripply bars and through still pools. It is called a creek in this country, not a brook (which would be a very small and brief thing), nor a river (which would be much larger). It is named, probably, from some Indian character or tribe, or from some old settler, or from the trees that dominate its margin—Walhonding, Scioto, Big Darby, Big Walnut.

The water, as you look down upon it from the bank, is translucent—not muddy in a dense way, nor crystal clear. Wherever they find conditions to their liking, clean, erect water-plants grow in ranks and patches. They are not the plants of stagnant water but are fresh and sweet and crisply vigorous.

You can wade much of the stream, and you will find the water midway between warm and cold. The rocks of the stream-bottom offer adventure. They look innocent. But their surface is more slippery than that of wet ice. No matter how certain you may be that you can place your foot where your step will be secure, there is always a lurking chance that you will suddenly sit down. When you have done so you will be inclined to remain for a while, enjoying the friendly, quietly flowing water.

If you wade you will see crayfish. As you disturb small rocks in the stream, near its margin or in the gravelly bars, a little gray-brown form will scuttle away, moving quickly, stern first, for a yard or two and skilfully backing into a new sheltering crevice, with only eyes and the ends of claws showing. The crayfish is past master at swift and adroit hiding.

In the long, still, irregular pools there are sometimes black bass. Unless the pool is a deep one you will not fool these fish with ordinary pole and line and bait, and they will have none of you if you so much as disclose the least part of yourself within remotest view. But stand far off in the stream bed, with fly-rod, with long silk line and invisible gut leader and tiny spinner-fly, and let your line descend gently through the air and your lure move skilfully through the water—and suddenly the still surface of the pool may be shattered by a jumping, plunging, fighting fish.

But no matter whether you fish or not, no matter whether you land a bass or not, the creek has much to offer. Kildeer call and circle. Little sand-pipers run along the shore. A heron flies lazily upstream. The ripples on the gravel bars glimmer in the sunlight. And the still pools mirror the big trees overhead.

A SUNSET CAPTURE

Cloud-form, do not hurry by!
Let my eyes in rapture
Watch your body when pale dye,
Loveliest in Nature,
Flooding upward, far and wide,
Sprite of hushed adventure,
Seeks with love to reach your side,
Eager for your capture.
Let me watch the primrose flush,
Breath of dying grandeur,
Flood your form with that brief blush
Only Love can conjure!

SIBELIUS

The second movement of the Sibelius Concerto in D Minor, played by Heifetz, is a powerful thing, sweeping in its intensity. It seems to be a deep and brave declaration of love, a love that is vital and perpetual. The composer, perhaps, was not expressing that thought in those measures, but that doesn't matter. That is what the music says to me.

FRIENDS

I saw a man standing close beside a bird in the Washington Zoo. The bird was just an ordinary green parrot in its cage, and the cage was one of many. The man was unprepossessing, and he was dressed in rough clothes. But the two, man and bird, were like two close and understanding friends.

The man was talking to the bird, but so softly that I could not understand what he said. He put a finger through the bars of the cage, and the bird took this in its hooked beak, but took it gently, carefully. Then the man put his cheek against the cage, and the bird pressed close, turning so that its head rested against the man's cheek, fairly lying down on its perch in its delight.

WITHOUT CHANGE

There is one thing that does not change with the passing of years and the coming of modern improvements. The smell of tea is just the same, and the smell of coffee, and the smell of all the other articles that grow in foreign countries. Fast steamships instead of sailing vessels may bring them here, and they may be hauled from the wharves in trucks, and they may have new trade names on their packages—but their aroma is eternal!

TO THE DAWN MOON

Waning Moon!
Dim and slender in the morning sky,
After you have shown the dawn the way,
Leading all the timid shades on high,
After you have brought the vivid day
Must you, wan, unnoticed, fade away?

TRADITION

I have been thinking about tradition—about the strong and lasting influence that it may have upon a community. In its potency it is like something possessed of life, something that takes on an attribute of immortality. Its power seems not to diminish with the passing of years but rather even to grow. It pervades human lives, moulds their outlooks and their interests, leads them in specific directions. It can be a stronger influence than that of a living person or group of persons. If it is embodied in the memory of some human being it can be more potent than that human being was when alive.

The mid-west city which I am visiting lives in an atmosphere of tradition. You would not anticipate this from its geographical location or its surroundings. In these respects it is not arrestingly different from various other cities of this part of the United States. Lushly fertile country borders it. Low hills and coal mines are not far away. Highways and railways radiate from it. Automobiles congregate in its broad, bare, central streets, as no doubt wagons and carriages did before them. A river curves broadly along its margin.

But on that river came explorers, very early in the settlement of the central part of the United States, and those explorers founded this city. Behind them they left a tradition—a record of historic achievement—a pervading influence that remains today a living thing in the life and activities and thoughts of the people, just as if the spirits of those venturesome, eager Frenchmen still occupied the houses and walked the streets. In the flesh they may have been very ordinary human beings—perhaps a little more daring, more visionary, than others. Dead, they are more than human.

Something similar must prevail in countless communities all over the earth. What some one man did, or some group of men, becomes in some way an undying influence.

I think that perhaps it is not among his friends that a man's life may count for most, but among those who follow later in the place where he lived and worked.

GRIEG

From the other room comes Grieg's "Concerto in A Minor." Nothing could bring a cooler, more refreshing, exhilirating close to an over-warm summer day. A night breeze has just brushed by me from my window, and it seems a part of the music.

DESENSITIZED

I was looking out of the window of my train a little while ago and, without being aware of them, I was seeing the branches of trees against the sky, fields of grasses, the smooth, round trunks of beech trees. When at last I became aware, I found that I had to make an effort to see these things with eyes of the spirit as well as the body. I had to hold and direct my attention. If I let go for a moment I lost them—all the real inner beauties, out there, within my spiritual grasp. I did not even know until this moment that there were flowing contours in the landscape that my window has been framing for the last half hour.

And so I have been thinking of the forces, of the pressures and responsibilities, that sometimes desensitize us; of what it means to us to be desensitized. We fall into ways in which we drive our hours—drive them so hard and so intensely that our inner spirits become worn and deadened. Nothing is left in them to respond to the exquisite values that are everywhere and always around us. The crowded hours leave no loophole to look out from. This afternoon as I was looking out of the window I was paying the penalty for such hours. That penalty is too high a price.

Work should never in the world operate to shut us off from the spiritual loveliness of the world about us. I think that we need to control the desensitizing forces of intense work and its contacts and effects, and I believe that to do so is the part of wisdom and rightness.

REFLECTIONS

When wading birds, reflected on a pool's calm face,
Pause, and each with poised and quiet step
Casts another picture in another place,
When no least wave distorts the mirrored wings,
When all is toned to mellow light,
When hunger waits until another hour
And no quick terror causes flight,
A quietude is born, unknown, unfelt before,
That sends an unseen shaft of silent Peace
To those of us who stand upon the shore.

When the younger members of a family have grown up, I believe that a continuance of the same daily, intimate contact of all the members of that family, including the younger, can sometimes be one of the most confusing, difficult things in the world. It is not always so with all people. There are some who are so constituted that everything seems to move placidly. Perhaps they have some welding trait in common. But for many, such contact means, I am sure, a baffling, disquieting way of living.

The thing is different when children are young. I suppose that during that period the younger members of a family are adjusted to a logical status because of the feeling that there is a natural authority over them, and their parents are adjusted to it because of their standing and obligation. Thus the unit is sound and right. But once the children are themselves adult, basic conditions are altered. If the same intimate contacts are then maintained, there can be strain and confusion.

The situation that results seems to have intricate elements. Solicitude on the part of one member of the family for another continues. It does not die out. Perhaps it even grows stronger because of greater knowledge of what can happen to a human being, and what ought to be done to avoid unfortunate happenings, and what ought to be done to bring about fortunate ends. But the one who feels the solicitude feels also a sort of responsibility and may feel a kind of proprietorship that colors everything done. When that happens, the one who is the object of solicitude resents the implication of inferior judgment or inadequate performance, and dislikes the proprietorship. Thus an ambition, when disclosed to other members of the family, seems to the one who holds it to be something that needs to be defended. It may appear to those who are told of it as something that might benefit by scrutiny. In the presence of family members, an achievement that is looked up to by friends comes to seem like something almost shabby, and so either is magnified in self-defense or is suppressed. Enthusiasm comes to look like rashness and to feel like foolishness. Everything is on a warped basis.

When all this prevails how can there be true valuation and how can there be the right sense of adjustment and the right understanding?

I believe it logical that these facts should often hold true. In our form of civilization a family is not supposed to continue as a closely knit unit. Each of its younger members is a new human being, who ought to fit into a new combination of conditions. His possibilities cannot be fully made realities unless that is done. As an adult person he may logically find among friends those who are in closest accord with his desires and aims. It is not always logical to expect as much anywhere else.

I think that sometimes we unduly worry because we do not find with brothers or sisters or parents as much in common as we find with close friends—or because with our own folk we feel what seems like a diminished bond. I believe that often the bond ought to diminish. It does so because, as each of us grows older, he becomes more and more definitely a new, individual human being.

SKY

The sky today—It is completely uneasy and restless and uncertain of its own future—Dark and light clouds crowding each other until they heap high to the zenith—And then everything drifts apart and a bit of blue shines through. I love the sky with all its clouds today and its occasional bit of laughter.

SOLACE

Mountain Peak, forsaken by my thoughts,
Banished by insistent hours of pain,
Deign to grant me altar space once more
Where thy sloping sides embrace the plain!

Let me stand as prodigal returned,
Paying homage with my paltry means!
Let me ask. . . And then do thou bestow
Benediction from thy still ravines!

HIGH SPOTS

These spots of pleasure in the course of the day! They stand out now like cool gusts of a grateful breeze—

—A moment when I washed my hands in the cold stream in front of my cabin and felt the clean, sparkling water flowing over my skin and through my fingers and around my wrists,

—A bright, widewake plant of forget-me-not, all decked in blossoms, growing in the midst of the gravel where I washed my hands. (Its feet must have been in the water itself. That same gravel was deeply covered with water early this Spring.)

—Thrushes singing in the deep woods.

—Mount Washington with its upper reaches buried in dark gray clouds that looked wild and elemental.

—Areas of woods so great and so many that this human race will never be able to harm them.

—A baby snowshoe rabbit—clearly not the usual baby rabbit at all—its legs very long and ungainly, its ears very tall. It crossed the road ahead of my car.

HUSH

Hush! Can you hear the languid lullaby
That memory murmurs to your listening mind,
The glorious blended music of each kind
Of lyric sound the world has offered to your ears
In all your living years?

Hush! Hear again the harmony of all
The birds once heard, each vivid, poignant call
In varied tones, so woven with the dawn,
The life, the death of days!—Faint notes that lingered on
To sing a memory song.

Hark to the tinkling sound on pebbly beach
That tides, once seen retreating far from reach,
Were wont to make when whitecapped, ebbing waves
Sped swiftly on to death and left sweet tunes behind
For memory to find.

Hear! Hear once more each softly blended chord
That all sweet passing days and nights record
In lasting, magic strains, as each hour dies!
The melody will sound for you, a blend of all
Swift time beyond recall.

HIDDEN

I held in my hand for several minutes this morning a long, slender, symmetrical, honeysuckle bud. It was tightly sealed. It showed no sign of beginning to open into the lacy honeysuckle flower. I do not think I have ever held anything so hidden, so secret, so protective of inner content, as this bud. After a time I became vandal and broke open the smooth white surface and laid bare its holy of holies. I should not have done this.

FIRES

In many parts of the world fires built by natives are very small, minute things, over which food can never be cooked with thoroughness. In some tropical countries small bamboo fires are made. In Ireland peat is burned in small quantities within fireplaces of scant depth. In the Arctic oil fires are used, and of necessity are restricted. On the Tibetan plateau yak-dung provides a fire of a kind, smoky and small. But here in this glorious country of ours we put logs—two and three foot logs—into our fireplaces, and watch them burn in lovely, high flames. We are lucky!

CRANES

This morning I stopped my car at a lowland pond where I know that two large, gray cranes live. I looked along the shore and over the water, not seeing them at first,—and then, from somewhere, they rose in flight, and behind them two children. It was a family picture of great beauty.

I hope that they all live on in peace there throughout the summer, unharmed, and that when Fall comes they will be well prepared for their long migration. I shall watch for them each time I pass their pond.

A SWAYING WORLD

For a long time yesterday afternoon I lay and watched the uppermost branches of the tall and slender trees back of my cabin.

A small bird had his hunting ground up there. There is a branch near the top of a maple where he perched, and from this he went forth in swift and intricate flights to other branches in other trees near by. I suppose that he was capturing insects too small for me to see. All of his surroundings were swaying and swinging in the breeze. Even when the wind seemed to cease, his tree and all the others were in motion. His whole world was constantly on the move. When a gust of wind came, the tree-tops swayed back and forth many feet.

I thought of the ground that we human beings walk on and live on and build our houses on, and of its contrast to the small bird's world. Everything that we do is dependent on a solid, immovable footing. If our ground were to sway an inch we'd be terror-stricken. If it were to move a foot, all our houses and factories and office-buildings would come tumbling down about our heads and crush us.

It seemed to me that human beings are not so remarkably clever. When we move we go in just one plane, always in contact with the earth—except for aircraft, which after all are only a fraction as efficient in flight as the birds or insects. We could no more adjust our activities to a world such as that of my bird than we could hop to the moon. We could not possibly build a durable home that swayed with the tree-tops, and build it with no tools at all. We are just stolid beings, fastened to a stolid earth.

I think that creatures that can live in a swiftly moving world, such as the tree-tops, must themselves be light of body, light of motion, and light of heart. No wonder birds sing!

Is it not to be expected, after all, that creatures living on the earth or in it—lesser creatures as well as greater—seldom lift their voices in song?

Is it not natural that sailors, old-time sailors, riding the cresting waves with the winds to carry them, had many a song?

Is it not natural that colored folk, old-time colored folk, living close to trees and birds and mystery, were forever singing?

138

EXALTATION

Let me halt one brimming wave
About to break upon some shore!
Let me quench one lightning flash
Amid the thunder's rolling roar!
Let me hush the wayward fall
Of one swift star across the night!
Let me pluck one beat of time
From madcap hours in milling flight!
Let me keep a rosebud young
When heart unfolding seeks its way!
Let me hold the robe of dawn
When dawn would flee the light-filled day!
Let me mingle but one breath
With power sublime, that I may be
So enriched by mystic light
The cosmic pulse will throb in me!

SEEDS

A continuous happening of yesterday delighted me. Seeds drifted constantly across the road and looked ethereally lovely in the sunlight. Once I stopped the car and pursued one as it drifted quietly along. I caught it and examined it with reverence for many moments. It was a tiny seed with an aura of white fluff. If I had not stopped it perhaps it would have been a lovely thing later on. After I had looked and examined it to my heart's content I should have put it carefully in the ground instead of tossing it away, with its fluff crushed down, into a place where it will have little chance of taking root.

ADVENTURERS

Yesterday chickadees came back. Where do you suppose that they have been all this time? I think that it must be two months, if not three, since any at all have been here. Have they been in nearby woods, busy with chickadee household affairs, and have they now raised their children for this season? Or have they been off to the mountains and to more northern regions?

One way or the other they must have had adventures since March or April. They could relate much, I am sure—journeys, nest-building, escapes from enemies, discoveries of food bounties, storms—a great story. I wish that it were possible to hear their tale.

QUIET LOVE

In the gray darkness of coming night
Your dear face, half pale in the thinning light,
Turned in the shadows to meet
My eyes—and that moment was sweet!

Smile answered smile and our breathing stirred
A little, perhaps. From our lips no word
Lessened the peace of the hour,
Diminished its passionless power.

Then from the dusk a new light arose!
Between us the spirit of white repose
Drifted—and there in the lea
Of night, quiet love came to me.

THE ILLIMITABLE VAULT

The sky is blue today, and the gray clouds that frame and border the blue only make it the deeper and richer and more vast. If the clouds were not there, perhaps we might forget for a moment that the illimitable vault of the blue is over all, that it stretches on and on beyond anything that you and I can know or can conceive, that it holds in its infinity a morning star and the wealth of all the worlds there are—sunshine—cosmic rays to light the way even in the darkest night!

BANK SWALLOWS

Yesterday I climbed a hill. Rushing up and down the slope of it, in their own wondrous way of flight, were hundreds of swallows. When I reached the top of the hill I found that the far side of it was a bare clay cliff, and there I found hundreds of swallow homes carved out of the bank.

CITY WEATHER

Apparently in a city it is difficult to have weather that is satisfactory. Almost any kind of weather that is original or individualistic or possessed of a way of its own is a misfortune. Rain is a wet and dismal nuisance, cold is something to hide away from, wind is a boisterous and dirty rowdy, and vigorous sunshine is too hot.

NOTHING CAN TAKE ITS PLACE

The restorative power of the woods and streams, the shrubs and wild plants, the earth and leaf mold! The strong trunks of the trees seem to bring strength to the human body and spirit. The tender beauty of bud and flower, of green moss and lichen, makes all the

ugliness of daily work and its problems vanish. The wind in the trees, the soft patter of rain-drops, the play of light on the rapids in a stream—all seem to push back the crowding world and make it retreat far away. Nothing, I think, can take the place of these things except only rare companionship. And that may be at its best when in the company of these elements.

No doubt there are countless persons to whom the untouched outdoor world makes no appeal that reaches to their consciousness. It represents only that which is crude or uncomfortable, which needs to be tamed, improved, dressed up. A fallen log should be removed and the place where it lay should be graded and smoothed over. A stream should have its banks straightened and sodded, or margined with a stone wall or with concrete. A tangle of drift-wood should be cleared away and arrangements made so that further tangles will not form. A slope too steep for a road should be cut down. Telephone lines should run everywhere, and power lines for radios, and there should be amusement centers and excursions to them each Sunday. Then and with sufficient crowds the place can serve.

But I think that somewhere, in most beings, somewhere beneath the habits and fears that cities and houses and herding together have fostered, there remains a response to that which was the environment of all human creatures a few short thousand years ago.

SEPARATION

Touched by the frail light of evening,
Cloaked in the folds of departure,
Stilled by thy leaving,
My timid love stoops—for thy blessing,
And droops—where thy footsteps are falling.

UNDER THE SKY

Sunshine glows softly today on the tops of pine trees. A beautiful day! The light is tempered, adjusted, refined, clear and not yet crystalline, softly pure and alluring. The air is neither dull nor intoxicating, but like the light is toned to a gentle purity.

WINTER COMES

A silver touch of frost,
Gleaming with cold and crystal light,
Making the dim world bright,
Seeking the grass, the rocks, the trees,
Frosting the waking morning breeze,
Ah, Frigid Breath, you're here!
Chilled are the lingering hours of night.

Stilled is the Summer's gentle life.
Sharp are your words, "Lush days, no more!
Bend for my icy cloak of hoar!"

BUNCH-BERRIES

My bunch-berries are boldly red on the slope of my knoll—vivid,
full, red berries, lush in the sunlight. It seems only an hour ago
that instead of berries there were white flowers. The wonder of a
season that hurries away!

TO WHAT UNCHARTED LANDS

You are the ardor of the day to me,
You are the gentleness of slumb'ring night,
You are the glory of the rising sea,
You are the freedom of the falcon's flight!
Yours is all that mystic, soaring power
That makes my lovefilled, newborn eyes behold
The very soul stuff of the smallest flower,
The very life-blood of a grain of gold.
Where will you lead—to what uncharted land?
I do but ask for joy of knowing where.
Perhaps to some far cloud-encircled strand
Where you will gather starlight for my hair!

CABIN

. . . . . . The beauty of all the world seems to creep into me as I
lie here before my mountain, seems to fill me with a strength and
power that must have utterance.

I have thought of large and costly places with gardens and
walks. There is not one in the world to compare with my cabin of
logs and my garden of wild flowers.

THE WRITTEN WORD

Is this not true—?
No matter what the experiences related or the scenes described
or the thoughts expressed, the spirit that flows beneath and through
the written word determines the quality of its life. If that spirit is
unvital or detached, the result will be something without vitality.
If it is that of friend to friend the quality of that friendship will be
there. And if it is the outpouring of one soul to another near and
dear soul, the living breath of that vital interchange will pervade
every particle of its substance, inevitably and unmistakably.

The poems in this book
and many of the briefer notes
are by
EDNA POMFRET LANE
1895–1940

Few who walk this earth live as rich a life as did Edna Pomfret Lane. On the material side—though she would not have counted that significant—her achievements were many. A graduate in the law she was a member of the Massachusetts bar. Possessed of marked administrative ability she successfully met executive responsibilities in two manufacturing corporations. But it is because of her spiritual qualities that her friends cherish her memory. Holding fast to extraordinarily high ideals she set for herself such standards as few attain, and in these she was potent inspiration for those who knew her.

Out of her quick imagination and her sensitive perceptions she wrote these poems, and some of the brief prose notes. She could not live to see them in permanent form, but in them her valiant spirit lives on, unchanged.

CPSIA information can be obtained at www.ICGtesting.com
Printed in the USA
BVOW08*0204161015

422745BV00002B/4/P

9 781258 106331